PASTOR JACKSON LAHMEYER

CHASING AFTER THE
WIND

WHY NOBODY IS CATCHING WHAT EVERYBODY IS CHASING

FOREWORD BY MAJOR LEAGUE GREAT
DARRYL STRAWBERRY

Chasing After The Wind:

ISBN: 979-8-9988247-0-8

Copyright © by Clay Clark

Clay Clark Publishing
3920 West 91st Street South
Tulsa, OK 74132

ACKNOWLEDGMENTS

This book is dedicated to my wife, Kendra, our five kids, Hannah, Ashton, Blitz, Eva and Laken, as well as the entire Sheridan.Church family. Thank you for supporting me while I have preached hundreds of sermons over the years that gave birth to this book.

I want to particularly thank Clay Clark who has been an advisor and a friend through many battles. Without Clay continually pressing me to write this book, it would not exist.

STATEMENTS ABOUT JACKSON LAHMEYER

"Jackson, I am proud of you!"
- **PRESIDENT DONALD J. TRUMP**
45th & 47th President of the United States, February 10, 2024

"It's amazing all that God is using Pastor Jackson and Sheridan.Church for in America."
- **PERRY STONE**
Evangelist & Best–Selling Author, September 8, 2024

"IMPRESSIVE. That is the word that comes to mind about Pastor Jackson."
- **ROBERT KIYOSAKI**
Author of Rich Dad, Poor Dad, March 6, 2025

"Pastor Jackson is a man of great character, strength and vision. I love his determination."
- **MAYOR RUDY GIULIANI**
Mayor of New York City, December 7, 2024

"Pastor Jackson is Central Casting for what a Pastor should be."
- **KASH PATEL**
Director of the FBI, September 11, 2023

"Pastor Jackson truly does not compromise and loves the Lord."
- **RABBI JONATHAN CAHN**
Best Selling Author, April 7, 2024

"If I was in a foxhole, I would want to be in it with Jackson Lahmeyer."
- **LT. GENERAL MICHAEL FLYNN**
Retired Three Star General in the US Army, March 21, 2022

"I just love what God is doing through Pastor Jackson in our country."
- **ERICK STAKELBECK**
Host of Stakelbeck Tonight, January 26, 2025

FOREWORD

BY: MLB LEGEND DARRYL STRAWBERRY

I won four World Series Championships. I was an eight-time MLB All-Star. I was the first overall pick in the 1980 draft and the National League Rookie of the Year. I had money, fame, women, cars, jewelry and success; everything that was supposed to make me happy. I was living the fast life, but I had a civil war taking place inside me. Nothing was able to satisfy my heart's desire to be happy, no matter how much "success" I had. Statistically, I was at the top of the mountain but in reality, I was at the very bottom of the valley in life. I was rich and famous but not a real man. I was trying to pursue happiness in everything and anything the world offered. This pursuit of happiness led me to being suspended three times by the MLB for substance abuse. I also found myself in prison and three million dollars in debt with no driver's license. When I hit rock bottom everyone that was once with me on the mountain top quickly scattered. But God...

My journey began in Los Angeles, California. I was a naturally gifted athlete and excelled in both basketball and baseball at Crenshaw High School. I was a 6'5 forward playing

High School basketball with a ferocious left-handed dunk. I could have gone to the next level in basketball, but baseball was my sweet spot. It came naturally and easily to me.

In High School, I played Right Fielder and was also a left-handed pitcher with a devastating curve ball, but my coaches warned against it because of the high possibility of injury to my throwing arm. However, it was in the batter's box that I truly flourished and later would become known for my "big swing." When I stepped up to the plate my mentality was, "I am the man!" This was not me being cocky, but I was very confident in my ability at bat. Although my baseball career was excelling, my home life was extremely dysfunctional.

I was raised by my mother, Ruby Strawberry, who was a Saint among Saints but my father was a raging alcoholic. One day he pulled a shotgun out and threatened to kill the entire family. My brothers and I responded and nearly killed him. I was broken. Even star athletes can be broken under the uniform. I covered my brokenness as best I could, but it led to bad decisions on my part. By the age of fourteen, I was smoking marijuana on a daily basis on the way to school and drinking alcohol after class. I got kicked out of four Junior High Schools for my behavior that I now know stemmed from the brokenness in my heart. My father beat me regularly and told me that I would never amount to anything at all.

Thankfully, I had several coaches who believed in me and became father-like figures in my life. These coaches in High School, the Minor Leagues and the Big Leagues all instilled in me discipline, preparedness, and a work ethic that pushed me to be one of the best baseball players to ever put on a Mets, Dodgers, Giants, or Yankees uniform. Although my number eighteen jersey might be retired at the Mets Field, I did not get there on my own. I had coaches, teammates and trainers who helped me along the way.

When I was on the field, I was in paradise, but off the field I was in turmoil and tried to fill the void with drugs, alcohol, women, and cars. I was wishy-washy in my faith like a lot of athletes who will thank God in the post-game interview but then end up at the club right after. This led to destruction in my life. I always say, "You can choose your sin but not your consequences."

In the midst of my addiction, I was blessed with a mom who was praying for me and my wife, Tracy, who was pulling me out of dope houses and bringing me to church. When I got real with God, I sat in church for seven years being discipled and God transformed me into a real man. I discovered my purpose was not baseball. Baseball was simply a platform. My purpose is to live for Christ and to tell others about how God is in the business of changing people just like me. The Gospel is about setting people free. I learned that happiness was never going to be found in success, awards, money or the fast life. Only in Christ is there true happiness. I tried everything the world had to offer but none of it satisfied my broken heart. I have found happiness because I am in Christ.

You have a purpose in this life. You can have real happiness as well. But take it from me that nothing the world offers you will actually make you happy. I have been there and done that and it does not work. However, the lessons in this book by Pastor Jackson Lahmeyer will show you how to discover true happiness and purpose which is found only in Jesus Christ.

-Darryl Strawberry | 4x World Series Champion

INTRODUCTION

Let me begin with a question: What is the one thing that everyone regardless of background, culture, or age truly desires in life and chases with all their might?

Think on this: the kid at the playground out playing with friends, the alcoholic at the dive bar, the single guy seeking a girl to match with online, the young woman contemplating suicide in her studio apartment, and the college student attending a frat party are all chasing the same thing, but through different pathways.

The answer to what all of the above people and everyone else are chasing is HAPPINESS. The child out on the playground believes that fun with friends is the ultimate happiness. The alcoholic at the dive bar believes just one more round will produce a state of euphoria to drown out the sorrows. The man looking for a wife online believes that marriage will fill the void of emptiness in his heart and bring forth joy. The young woman contemplating suicide cannot escape the despair of life and therefore thinks that ending her own life will place her in a state of eternal bliss. And the college student at the frat party is convinced that an all nighter of pleasure will fulfill the heart's desire of simply being happy. Everyone is pursuing happiness, but nobody seems to be able to catch it, much like *chasing after the wind.*

"If I were to ask, why have you believed in Christ, why you have become Christians, every man will answer truly, 'For the sake of happiness'"
– Augustine of Hippo[1]

[1.] Augustine of Hippo is considered one of the most influential Christian leaders in Church history. His timeless book *"The Confessions"* is one of the most read Christian books of all time.

FROM THE AUTHOR

First, I realize from answering the question at the beginning of this book that many will assume it contains nothing more than the equivalent of spiritual cocaine, which will give you as the reader a quick high, but produce no real lasting impact after the book has been placed back on the shelf. Let me assure you that the contents of this book are the exact opposite. A spiritual high that quickly wears off will not be the result, but through the power of the Holy Spirit, I am convinced the scriptural revelation and the practical insights found in this book will change your life as it did and still is changing mine.

Secondly, I recognize there are a few modern American Christians who do not like to use the words "happy" or "happiness" to describe the Christian experience, but prefer the use of the word "joy" instead. I am choosing to use the words "happy" and "happiness" throughout this book, not according to a modern meaning of a subjective feeling, but according to how the ancients viewed and used the words "happy" and "happiness". The great thinkers of Western Civilization such as Aristotle[2,] Augustine, Thomas Aquinas[3], Blaise Pascal[4], Jonathan Edwards[5], and C.S. Lewis[6] all used the words "happy" and "happiness" to mean an objective state of being. Dr. Peter Kreeft[7], professor of Philosophy at Boston College, summarizes what the ancients meant by happy/happiness: "(1) a state of real perfection (2) of soul (3) in complete life, including eternity. Aristotle's word for this was *eudaimonia*: the lasting state (*-ia*) of true goodness (*eu-*) of soul (*daimon*)." Therefore, since the most brilliant minds of Western Civilization all used the words "happy" and "happiness" then I too shall use these terms (happy and happiness) to be interchangeable with joy and pleasure.

Thirdly, defining what it means to be happy in life is as simple as asking lightning to be still in the sky for a picture. I relate the understanding of being happy to the understanding of the Incarnation of Christ (God becoming man). Much like the Incarnation, being happy is a mystery to be lived out and realized in real life, rather than a puzzle to be solved in a scientific lab. I believe that throughout the journey of this book, you may not be able to come up with a satisfactory dictionary definition to pass a college course on what happiness is, but you will be able to know in your own soul what it is to be truly happy and be able to say with all sincerity "*it is well with my soul*," which is God's desire for your life.

Lastly, The Ultimate Practical Guide To Happiness at the end of this book is the realistic nuts and bolts of how to achieve the high and lofty concepts that will be presented. One could easily argue that it is the most important portion of the book.

[2.] Aristotle was an ancient Greek philosopher with an influence that is hardly matched by any other philosopher.

[3.] Thomas Aquinas was the foremost Scholastic thinker of the Medieval Period, as well as one of the most influential philosophers and theologians in the history of Christianity.

[4.] Blaise Pascal was a French mathematician, physicist, inventor, philosopher, and theologian.

[5.] Jonathan Edwards was an American pastor and theologian during the 18th Century. Edwards is considered one of America's most important founding figures.

[6.] Clive Staples Lewis was a British writer and theologian. He was a professor of English literature at both Oxford and Cambridge.

[7.] Kreeft, Peter. 1993. *Christianity for Modern Pagans: Pascal's Pensées Edited, Outlined, and Explained.* Ignatius Press.

CONTENTS

CONTENTS

HAPPINESS LEADS TO HOLINESS

CHAPTER 1

It has been preached many times from behind differing pulpits that *"God does not want you happy, but instead He wants you holy."* This phrase is proclaimed as if there is some inherent choice of one or the other: either happiness in life or holiness in life. While that sounds spiritual like choosing between being a Christian Saint or an American Playboy, it is very antithetical to the Scriptures and the heart of God.

True: God wants you holy.

Also True: God wants you happy.

The two (happiness and holiness) are not incompatible partners like oil and water. In fact, the paradox of happiness and holiness is a beautiful blend in the life of a believer that is an absolute necessity to live the successful Christian life and truly become the Saint each of us are meant to be. Happiness and holiness in life are not an *either/or* but a *both/and*. **The key to a holy life is to live from a happy heart**. Without a happy heart it is impossible to live a holy life. Therefore, we should pursue true happiness so that we can live out authentic holiness.

This concept (happiness leads to holiness) has been described amongst those high in the ivory tower of the Theological Academy as *Christian Hedonism*[8]. If you are anything like me then those two words together make you a little uncomfortable. I remember the first time I heard these two words (Christian + Hedonism) together as a student at Oral Roberts University, I was more than perplexed. Here I was studying all kinds of new theological terms and concepts yet this concept caught my attention. In my mind at the time, a Christian Hedonist sounded like the epitome of an oxymoron, much like the expressions: "*wise fool*" or "*pretty ugly*".

True: God wants you holy.

Also True: God wants you happy.

Initially, I did not think that being a Christian Hedonist was legitimate. However, I have walked with the Lord and fought

8. See, Piper, John. 1996. Desiring God: Meditations of a Christian Hedonist. Multnomah Books.

my own sinful appetites and desires not just as a Christian but as a Pastor nonetheless, and I have discovered that living a holy life as much as I want to is really, really difficult. In fact, for me… it has been impossible. I have found myself astonished with my own thoughts, attitudes, words and behaviors not just before I was a Christian but after becoming one and even while being used by God in the ministry. The great Reformer, Martin Luther said two things that I have found to be accurate and true about myself.

1. **"Before I was a Christian, I was a slave to sin, and I fought against God. Now that I am a Christian, I am a slave to God, but I still fight against sin."**
– Martin Luther[9]
2. **"The old me was drowned with water baptism, but that bastard is one good swimmer."** – Martin Luther

I can testify and verify that the *"old Jackson"* is an Olympic caliber swimmer on the level of Michael Phelps and Katie Ledecky. For so many years I wanted to live right. I preached good and honest sermons to others that they needed to live right but all the while my heart cried out the timeless words of the

[9] Martin Luther is best known for leading the Protestant Revolution during the 16th Century in Germany,

Apostle Paul, "**I do not understand what I do. For what I want to do I do not do, but what I hate I do**" (Romans 7:15).

If the words of the Apostle Paul and Martin Luther ring true for you in your soul, then this is the right book for you. If you have already reached sinless perfection and total happiness, then dare not read any further or I might completely mess up your supercilious spirituality and I would not want to do that (C.S. Lewis once said, "*spiritual pride is the most beautiful vice in hell*").

Since you have made it this far, let me present to you what I have discovered although it is not original to me, but has been taught by the likes of Paul, Augustine, Pascal, Lewis, and many of the other brilliant thinkers throughout the storied history of the Church. Here it is: *You and I were created to be happy and holy.* Until our hearts find happiness, our lives will continually fall into unholiness. Therefore, seek and find happiness to live out a life of holiness.

The problem we all run into is that we easily settle for things that never give us true and lasting happiness. Unless your heart finds true happiness, you will never live out authentic holiness. Let me give you an example from the Bible.

King Solomon was the wisest man to ever live and was extremely successful as the 3rd King of Israel (*Saul then David then Solomon*). Under Solomon, Israel experienced geographical growth, an economic boom and peace with her enemies. Solomon had everything that power, wealth and fame could attain. Yet, although Solomon was wise, wealthy, healthy, and prosperous, he lived a very unholy life. Hear the Word of the Lord to Solomon:

> **"The Lord became angry with Solomon because his heart had turned away from the Lord, the God of Israel, who had appeared to him twice. [10] Although he had forbidden Solomon to follow other gods, Solomon did not keep the Lord's command. [11] So the Lord said to Solomon, "Since this is your attitude and you have not kept my covenant and my decrees, which I commanded you, I will most certainly tear the kingdom away from you and give it to one of your subordinates. [12] Nevertheless, for the sake of David your father, I will not do it during your lifetime. I will tear it out of the hand of your son."**

> \- 1 Kings 11:9-12

Why did Solomon live so unholy when he had been given divine wisdom, incredible wealth and unparalleled success? The answer is simple. Solomon lived an unholy life because Solomon had a very unhappy heart.

One of the most interesting, yet sometimes disturbing books in the Bible is the Book of Ecclesiastes. This book is different from all the other books in the Bible. It is written by Solomon in his old age as he reflects on his life.

Solomon opens the book up like this: **"The words of the Teacher, son of David, king in Jerusalem: 2 "Meaningless! Meaningless!" says the Teacher. "Utterly meaningless! Everything is meaningless"** (Ecclesiastes 1:1-2). Talk about being a real "debbie-downer". The wisest man to ever live concludes at the end of his life that everything in life is meaningless. So why is this book in the Bible? The word meaningless here is often translated as vanity, but the word really means vapor in Hebrew. Think of a soap bubble, one moment it is there and the next it is gone. This thought of Solomon leads to his own autobiography in chapter two of Ecclesiastes.

"I said to myself, "Come now, I will test you with pleasure to find out what is good." But that also proved to be meaningless. 2 "Laughter," I said, "is madness. And what does pleasure accomplish?" 3 I tried cheering myself with wine,

and embracing folly—my mind still guiding me with wisdom.
I wanted to see what was good for people to do under the
heavens during the few days of their lives. ⁴ I undertook great
projects: I built houses for myself and planted vineyards. ⁵ I
made gardens and parks and planted all kinds of fruit trees
in them. ⁶ I made reservoirs to water groves of flourishing
trees. ⁷ I bought male and female slaves and had other slaves
who were born in my house. I also owned more herds and
flocks than anyone in Jerusalem before me. ⁸ I amassed silver
and gold for myself, and the treasure of kings and provinces.
I acquired male and female singers, and a harem as well—
the delights of a man's heart. ⁹ I became greater by far than
anyone in Jerusalem before me. In all this my wisdom stayed
with me. ¹⁰ I denied myself nothing my eyes desired; I refused
my heart no pleasure. My heart took delight in all my labor,
and this was the reward for all my toil. ¹¹ Yet when I surveyed
all that my hands had done and what I had toiled to achieve,
everything was meaningless, a chasing after the wind;
nothing was gained under the sun."

- Ecclesiastes 2:1-11

Solomon tried everything that life had to offer. He refused
himself nothing. He tried to find happiness in alcohol, but it
failed. He tried to find happiness in larger-than-life building
projects such as the Temple and the King's Palace, but it failed.
He tried finding happiness by having sex with countless women,
but it too failed. While Solomon was behaving so unholy, he

is clear to say that his wisdom never left him. How can one be so wise yet behave so poorly? The answer is simple: because Solomon was so unhappy, he behaved so unholy. Solomon had the head knowledge, but his heart was ever restless. He concludes his misery with these words: **"So I hated life, because the work that is done under the sun was grievous to me. All of it is meaningless, a chasing after the wind"** (Ecclesiastes 2:17).

This is why I agree with the wise words of the great Catholic theologian and philosopher, Thomas Aquinas: **"Man cannot live without joy. That is why it is necessary that a man depraved of spiritual joys goes over into carnal pleasures."** The reason that you and I struggle with sin and fall for temptation is simple: *We long to be happy and because we are unhappy, we are willing to do unholy things to try and find happiness.* **Our unholy behavior is a product of our unhappy heart.** The reason our hearts are unhappy is that we settle for things that promise happiness (sex, wealth, power, etc.), but the feeling of happiness only lasts for but a vapor.

The sad reality of humanity is that we settle for soap bubbles, and we chase the wind all our lives while never actually catching it. As long as we keep settling, we will continue to be unhappy and as long as we are unhappy, we will continue to behave unholy. I believe American Christians behave in such unholy ways because American Christians are extremely unhappy. This I know from first-hand experience as well as numerous credible surveys[10].

Let me mention here that if you are still skeptical about the importance of being happy then it might be helpful to realize that God is the happiest Being there is, and God does only that which makes Him happy. Psalm 115:3 shows this clearly: "**Our God is in heaven; He does whatever pleases Him**." God is happy and God is holy simultaneously.

The purpose of this book is two-fold. First, to show you that happiness in Christ should be your ultimate pursuit. Second, to help you discover how to be happy in Christ. This is not to say that I have fully reached this place because that would be a lie. However, I am on the pursuit and on this journey through much study, prayer and sermon preparation. I believe I have picked up on a few things that may be helpful for you like it has been for me.

"Our hearts are restless, until they can find rest in You."
– Augustine of Hippo

---

[10] See, "Americans Are Unhappier Than Ever | the World Happiness Report." 2025. March 20, 2025. https://worldthappiness.report/.

THE PROBLEM OF EVIL

CHAPTER 2

"For the joy set before Him, Christ endured the cross"
– Hebrews 12:2

How can anyone truly be happy in this life when it is filled with so many heartaches and headaches? The Bible describes this bleak reality in Job 14:1: **"Mortals, born of women, are of few days and full of trouble."** Although pain in life is inevitable, with Christ as the model we will discover that through great suffering comes greater happiness even what one could describe as *joy unspeakable*. It is true that there may be pain in the night, but joy does come in the morning (Psalm 30:5).

However, a very tough and honest question is: How can a good God that desires for His people to be happy allow so much pain and suffering? We might be headed towards the "sweet by and by" but we live in the "painful now and now."

There are many good arguments to prove the existence of God such as Intelligent Design or First Cause. Yet, an interesting truth is that the Bible never tries to prove the existence of God. The Bible assumes that the reader has enough common sense to realize that there must be a God. Psalms 14:1 says, **"Only the fool says in his heart, 'There is no God.'"** Atheism is much more a heart issue than a head issue; it is more about attitude than intellect. Ninety-nine percent of all human beings who have ever lived have believed in a God or gods. Why is that the case? Simply because believing in God is common sense. Although the Bible never tries to prove the existence of God, what it does do is describe who the true God is and what He is like.

The Bible paints a portrait of God in a manner that we who are *finite* can somewhat understand and comprehend He who is *infinite*. Scripture informs us that God is *omnipotent* (all-powerful), God is *omniscient* (all-knowing), God is *omnipresent* (ever-present), and God is omnibenevolent (all-good). If God is all these *omni*-s that Scripture describes then there is only one good argument against the existence of an all-powerful, all knowing, ever-present and all-good God. That argument is the undeniable existence of evil, pain and suffering. The famous question of every atheist and skeptic is: "Why would a good God who is all-powerful allow such bad things to happen to good people that He loves?"

Priests, philosophers, psychologists, and ordinary people have wrestled for centuries with the reality of the existence of evil, pain and suffering in our world because nobody is exempt from experiencing their disastrous and catastrophic effects. It is beyond challenging to witness a newly married couple with bright stars in their eyes living their dream of soon becoming parents only to wake up to the nightmare of a miscarriage. Why did an all-powerful and all-good God allow such a tragedy? Tragic examples like this are unfortunately endless in our troubled world. Because of this state that we all find ourselves in, we naturally search for answers as to why. Thankfully, there is an entire book in the Bible dedicated to addressing this complex problem. It is the Book of Job, which is all about a good man, better yet a great man who experienced a slew of terrible things in life through no fault of his own.

THE LIFE OF JOB

The Book of Job gives us the answer to the classic problem, which is the existence of evil and its undesirable offspring named pain, suffering, and death. If we believe that the Bible is the Word of God, then it is in the Book of Job that we are given the closest answer to this daunting problem by none other than God Himself. The theological term for this is *theodicy*.

"In the land of Uz there lived a man whose name was Job. This man was blameless and upright; he feared God and shunned evil."

– Job 1:1

We are introduced to the main character of the story in a very interesting way. Although we cannot be certain, it is believed that the land of Uz was somewhere in northern Arabia possibly near modern day Damascus. What we are told about the man Job is astonishing, to say the least. He was blameless and upright, and that he feared God and shunned evil. In other words, Job was a great man; he was a genuine Saint. There are some who try to say that the reason Job experienced great suffering was because he had some hidden sin in his life, which was the argument that the three friends of Job used later in the book. However, Job's suffering as we will see had nothing to do with sin in Job's life. We are told by the author that Job was blameless and upright. Not only does the author describe Job that way but so does God who knows everything about each of us, including Job.

"Then the Lord said to Satan, 'Have you considered my servant Job? There is no one on earth like him; he is blameless and upright, a man who fears God and shuns evil."

– Job 1:8

Both God and the author describe Job in the exact same manner. Therefore, we can be confident that Job did not suffer because of hidden sin in his life. We must take the author and God at their word in the description of the character of Job. Not only was Job a Saint, but he was also extremely blessed.

"He had seven sons and three daughters, and he owned seven thousand sheep, three thousand camels, five hundred yoke of oxen and five hundred donkeys, and had a large number of servants. He was the greatest man among all the people of the East."

– Job 1:2-3

Job is the ideal type of person that we all should strive to be. He was a godly man, with a large family, great professional success, and the respect of his community. Job was blessed with a large family; he had ten children. In ancient times, unlike our skewed postmodern world, children were always considered a blessing rather than a burden. He was also a prolific businessman. With three thousand camels, Job was in what we would call the trucking business today. His camels would have been rented and used to transport goods all over the ancient near east. The five hundred oxen would have plowed the fields of Job to plant seeds to grow food to sell, and the five hundred donkeys would have produced the delicacy of his day which was donkey milk. Up to this point, everything in Job's life from the outside was wonderful. However, Job was unaware of what was taking place in the spiritual realm, and we are much like Job in that we too are very unaware of what is taking place in the spiritual realm behind the scenes before it ever manifests on the stage in the natural world.

"One day the angels came to present themselves before the Lord, and Satan also came with them. [7] The Lord said to Satan, 'Where have you come from?' Satan answered the Lord, 'From roaming throughout the earth, going back and forth on it.'"
– Job 1:6-7

This imagery of the angels presenting themselves before the Lord is consistent with Jacob's dream of the stairway to heaven upon which he saw the angels ascend and descend in Genesis 28. One slight difference here in Job from Jacob's dream is that Satan presented himself to the Lord in heaven as well. It is here that we are given more detailed information about our enemy (*the Dragon, Serpent of Old, Devil and/or Satan*) than any other place in the Bible.

> **"Then the Lord said to Satan, 'Have you considered my servant Job? There is no one on earth like him; he is blameless and upright, a man who fears God and shuns evil.' ⁹ 'Does Job fear God for nothing?' Satan replied. ¹⁰ 'Have you not put a hedge around him and his household and everything he has? You have blessed the work of his hands, so that his flocks and herds are spread throughout the land.¹¹ But now stretch out your hand and strike everything he has, and he will surely curse you to your face.'"**
>
> **– Job 1:8-11**

What incredible insights we are given into the mysterious workings of the heavenlies. We are taken behind the scenes of Job's life and are given a glimpse into a conversation between God and Satan that unbeknownst to Job was taking place about him. Here we discover that our enemy has a unique intellect and will. God's question to Satan about Job is more of a rhetorical question of God saying to Satan: "I know you have been studying my servant, Job." We are told in Revelation 12:10 that Satan accuses the people of God, like Job, day and night. What does Satan accuse us of? Our past, our motives and where our hearts are. Satan essentially told God that the only reason that Job served Him was because of how good God had been to him.

"The Lord said to Satan, "Very well, then, everything he has is in your power, but on the man himself do not lay a finger." Then Satan went out from the presence of the Lord."

- Job 1:12

A hard truth that we must take away from this interaction is that Satan can do nothing without the permission of God first. Satan is on God's leash like a pitbull on the leash of its owner. This is a difficult reality to wrestle with, but a reality, nonetheless. If God is good, then why does God allow Satan to ruin Job's life? It is here in the story that Satan unleashed hell on earth in the Job's life. In one moment, Job went from having everything to complete devastation. All of Job's assets (oxen, donkeys, sheep, camels & servants) were either destroyed by natural disasters, or stolen by raiders. To make matters worse, a massive wind struck

10. See, "Americans Are Unhappier Than Ever | the World Happiness Report." 2025. March 20, 2025. https://worldhappiness.report/.

the house where all ten of Job's children were and none of his children survived. In one setting, Job lost all ten of his children and all the wealth he had accumulated over many years. I cannot even imagine this type of pain and suffering. Yet, here is the response of Job:

> **"At this, Job got up and tore his robe and shaved his head. Then he fell to the ground in worship** [21] **and said:'Naked I came from my mother's womb, and naked I will depart. The Lord gave and the Lord has taken away;may the name of the Lord be praised.'** [22] **In all this, Job did not sin by charging God with wrongdoing."**
> – Job 1:20-22

What a remarkable and stunning response. Truthfully, I cannot say with confidence that would have been my response; I probably would have screamed and sobbed. But this is further evidence that Job is truly a Saint. Notice the author is clear to present to us that Job did not sin in his words. Once again, we are being reassured that Job's suffering is not a result of sin in Job's life. You can imagine how puzzled and frustrated Satan must have been with the response from Job. He was convinced that Job would curse God, but instead Job did the exact opposite and blessed God. It is as if God knew something about Job that

Satan did not. Although Satan lost round one, we learn that our enemy is very persistent. The Devil is no quitter.

WHEN IT RAINS, IT POURS

"On another day the angels came to present themselves before the Lord, and Satan also came with them to present himself before him. ² And the Lord said to Satan, 'Where have you come from?' Satan answered the Lord, 'From roaming throughout the earth, going back and forth on it.' ³ Then the Lord said to Satan, 'Have you considered my servant Job? There is no one on earth like him; he is blameless and upright, a man who fears God and shuns evil. And he still maintains his integrity, though you incited me against him to ruin him without any reason.'"

– Job 2:1-3

Once again, God reaffirmed what we already knew about Job; he was a Saint. And most importantly that Job was suffering through no fault of his own.

"'Skin for skin!' Satan replied. 'A man will give all he has for his own life. ⁵ But now stretch out your hand and strike his flesh and bones, and he will surely curse you to your face.' ⁶ The Lord said to Satan, 'Very well, then, he is in your hands; but you must spare his life.'"

– Job 2:4-6

Satan told God, "Job may have lost his wealth, but let's be real. He still has his health, and with that he can regain his wealth. He may have lost his children, but he and his wife could have more children because Job is a healthy man." Satan said, "Let me hit him where it counts. Let me attack him where he will feel it the most. Yeah, he is hurting emotionally but let's see how Job responds with physical, nagging, relentless pain. Skin for skin and Job will surely curse you to your face." You can hear the murderous rage in the Devil's voice. There is a real Devil out there and he wants to destroy you; he is roaming around like a lion looking for anyone he can devour. But he cannot touch you without God's permission, and remember God knows what He is doing even if it does not make sense to us at the moment as I am sure it did not make any sense to Job.

"So Satan went out from the presence of the Lord and afflicted Job with painful sores from the soles of his feet to the crown of his head. ⁸ Then Job took a piece of broken pottery and scraped himself with it as he sat among the ashes. ⁹ His wife said to him, 'Are you still maintaining your integrity? Curse God and die!' ¹⁰ He replied, 'You are talking like a foolish woman. Shall we accept good from God, and not trouble?' In all this, Job did not sin in what he said."

– Job 2:7-10

How quickly the scene has shifted from Job's once blissful and blessed life, to now total wreckage and carnage. He lost his children, his wealth and now his health. He finds himself sitting among the "ashes" which is the G-rated version of the Hebrew word here for "dung" or the highly sophisticated S-word of our day... To make a terrible situation even worse, Job's wife told him to give up and just curse God so that he could die. Yet, once again we see how Job was truly a Saint. Amid all that he just experienced, he uttered a phrase that I am sure shook the Devil to his core: "Shall we accept good from God, and not trouble?" The entire premise that the Devil was working upon was that Job would only accept good things from God, but that if God would pull the good things from him then surely Job would curse God. The Devil was dead wrong, again. God knew something about Job that the Devil did not. God won the wager that the Devil presented. Job might have lost everything that he had, but he did not curse God, instead he blessed God in the middle of his pain and suffering.

BUT WHY GOD?

So far, we have seen a great man, Job, go through the unimaginable, yet withstand it in a way that is beyond impressive.

Although Job maintained his integrity through it all, there is no doubt that Job had to wonder, "*Why is God allowing these terrible things to happen to me?*" I have discovered, as a Pastor, in walking through difficult and painful situations with individuals and families, that once the tragedy is over, the most difficult hurdle is the question: "WHY?" Most of us can comprehend and process that if we do something wrong such as lie, cheat, or steal, and we experience something bad because of it, well that we can make sense of. But what about when you do not cause the pain or the suffering, yet you experience it anyway? We know that in the case of Job that his life getting turned upside down was not his fault. So why did God allow this?

It is human nature to feel the need to blame someone or something when a tragedy takes place. Recall the time the Pharisees brought a man who had been born blind to Jesus and asked who was to blame. Did his parents sin or did the man sin in his mother's womb causing him to be born blind? The Pharisees did what most of us do, tried to find blame. But Jesus baffled them when he said "neither... in fact, the man was born blind so that God would be glorified." That answer does not make sense to us, because in our finite minds, there must be someone or something to blame for the man being born blind.

GOOD FRIENDS. BAD COUNSELORS

This desire to discover blame for a tragedy was true in the days of Job as well. We see it when three of Job's friends arrive to comfort him and counsel him through his situation. The three friends might have been good friends with noble intentions, but they were terrible counselors with an awful bed-side manner. To be clear, the three friends were not bad people, and they do not even really have bad theology in comparison to the rest of the Bible. The friends are sincere in what they share with Job as they truly do care for him, but they are sincerely wrong. They are the typical "Monday-Morning-Quarterbacks."

Given that this book is not a commentary on the Book of Job, I will not bore you by covering in great length the thirty-five chapters of poetic conversation between Job and his three friends about why he was suffering. Instead, I will give a short summary of the conversation in a much less poetic and hopefully not-so-boring fashion.

Friend #1 – Eliphaz the Temanite. The name Eliphaz means "*God is victorious*." We hardly are given any information about him other than that he was a Temanite, a group of people known for their wisdom in the ancient world. It is believed that he is the oldest of the three friends and is by far the kindest of the three.

However, he preaches a sermon to Job in chapters 4-14 based on the philosophy that if you are truly godly then you will never suffer. He told Job, in not so few words, that he must have sinned and was therefore being punished by God. This type of thinking makes sense and is even supported throughout the Bible: if we obey God, He promises to bless us, but if we disobey Him, He promises to punish us (see Deuteronomy 28). The only problem with this line of thinking is that we have "inside-baseball" about Job; he was a genuine Saint, not a rebellious sinner.

Friend #2 – Bildad the Shuhite. The name Bildad means "*son of Hadad*." Like Eliphaz, we are given no substantive information about him. It seems he is the second oldest of the three and he delivered three speeches to Job in chapters 8, 18, and 25. Bildad reaffirmed everything that Eliphaz said, but added salt to Job's wound and injury to insult by stating that Job's children died because they must have sinned (Job 8:1-4). However, there is no indication in Scripture that the whirlwind that killed Job's children was due to sin in their lives.

Friend #3 – Zophar the Naamathite. The name Zophar means "*young bird*." It is mostly likely that he is the youngest of the three friends and definitely the harshest. He had very little patience for Job and his defense of himself against the slew of accusations. Zophar focused on the idea that Job must have been hiding sin because of all the terrible things that had happened to him.

During the rapid-fire poetic exchange of accusations hurled at Job, he tried to defend himself to no avail and nearly reached the edge of the cliff. He essentially told God that he wanted to go to court and argued that if his case were heard by an unbiased judge, the ruling would be in his favor. But Job quickly acknowledged that God is the judge and there would be no point in going to court (Job 9). For nearly thirty-five chapters, the friends of Job theologized and talked about God. Job, on the other hand, defended himself before his friends, but unlike the friends who only talked about God, Job talked directly to God trying to get a reason for why he was suffering without just cause. Finally, after everyone shut up... God showed up.

GOD ANSWERS JOB

"Then the Lord spoke to Job out of the storm. He said: [2] "Who is this that obscures my plans with words without knowledge? [3] Brace yourself like a man; I will question you, and you shall answer me. [4] "Where were you when I laid the earth's foundation? Tell me, if you understand. [5] Who marked off its dimensions? Surely you know! Who stretched a measuring line across it?"

– Job 38:1-6

Wow. Job, who originally was the questioner, became the one being questioned. God took Job through a series of rhetorical questions, clearly meant to highlight the vast difference between God and Job in stature, wisdom, nature, power, and knowledge. God quickly reminded Job that He is God and Job was not. This is something we all need to be reminded of periodically.

"The Lord said to Job: ² "Will the one who contends with the Almighty correct him? Let him who accuses God answer him!" ³ Then Job answered the Lord: ⁴ "I am unworthy—how can I reply to you? I put my hand over my mouth. ⁵ I spoke once, but I have no answer— twice, but I will say no more." ⁶ Then the Lord spoke to Job out of the storm: ⁷ "Brace yourself like a man; I will question you, and you shall answer me. ⁸ "Would you discredit my justice? Would you condemn me to justify yourself?"

- Job 40:1-8

After God took Job through several chapters of interrogation and questioning without ever directly answering Job's question - it was finally time for Job to respond.

"Then Job replied to the Lord: ² "I know that you can do all things; no purpose of yours can be thwarted. ³ You asked, 'Who is this that obscures my plans without knowledge?' Surely, I spoke of things I did not understand, things too

wonderful for me to know. ⁴ "You said, 'Listen now, and I will speak; I will question you, and you shall answer me.' ⁵ My ears had heard of you but now my eyes have seen you."

- Job 42:1-5

The answer to the problem of evil is: **WE DO NOT KNOW.** God never directly answered Job's question. It was and still is a mystery. If the Book of Job teaches us anything, there are some mysteries reserved for God alone. Life is much like the Incarnation (God becoming man). Life is a mystery to be lived rather than a puzzle to be solved. God does not give Job an answer about the problem of evil; instead, God gave Job something far greater: Himself.

God did not answer the questions in Job's head, but God fulfilled the deepest desire of Job's heart. Job 42:5 says, "**My ears had heard of you but now my eyes have seen you.**" The human heart longs to see the face of God. Job's reward for everything he had endured was this: he transitioned from simply hearing about God of the universe to seeing Him and knowing Him. Job thought he wanted an explanation from God about his undeserved suffering. Instead, he realized what he truly wanted all along was to see God face to face.

The summary of the Book of Job is this: God is not a character in our story, but we are a character in His. He is the Creator, and we are His creation. He is God, and we are not. God is the "I" and we are the "thou." For endless chapters, Job's three friends tried to get him to repent of some hidden sin. But, the only thing Job repented of was his trying to play God and trying to force an answer out of Him. Although he never got the answer he was seeking, Job became totally satisfied when God revealed Himself. Why? Because Job discovered the meaning of life: **TO SEE GOD**.

Job 42:12 is the icing on the cake, **"The Lord blessed the latter part of Job's life more than the former part."**

GLAD WHEN IT IS BAD

Is it possible to be happy even when life is hard? The answer is yes. The reason we can be happy during our times of suffering is because God shows up in an extraordinary way in our pain. C.S. Lewis said, "God whispers to us in our pleasure but He shouts to us in our pain." Our pain has a purpose. What's more important than what is happening to us is what is happening in us and through us. Paul says in Romans 8:28, **"And we know that in all things God works for the good of those who love him, who**

have been called according to his purpose." All things mean all things - the good, bad, and ugly.

Therefore, I may not know the reason why I am suffering, but I am thankful I can know the end result. The result is God's purpose for my life is being accomplished. It may not be my preference but like Job, God's purpose is being fulfilled. God knows how to weave everything together from the good to the bad to the ugly to the beautiful to the painful; He weaves it all into a beautiful story, which is your life and my life. He who began a good work in each of us is faithful to complete it. God has a unique ability to bring beauty from the ashes of tragedy.

Hardships in life are inevitable, but through pain we often find purpose. In 2021, I made a life-changing decision. I decided to run for the U.S. Senate in the state of Oklahoma against an incumbent Republican Senator. That meant I had a 99% chance of losing that race. However, I felt compelled to do it, and others agreed I should. For fifteen months, I crisscrossed the state of Oklahoma, and worked eighteen-hour days while still being a Pastor. Our campaign gained huge momentum with the support of General Michael Flynn, Sebastian Gorka, Mayor Rudy Giuliani, Roger Stone, and so many others. We became a viable threat to the sitting Senator. At the end of the day, we fell short and lost that race. I was personally devastated because of the amount of time, energy, and money not only I put forth, but also thousands of others who were behind me. I felt like I let them all down.

It is hard to describe what it is like to lose a political campaign. I had never experienced anything like it before since that night. Once the results were in, my wife and I went to the platform to address our supporters and I did not prepare a speech for a loss because I believed we were going to win. When I got up to speak, I was embarrassed and disappointed, but I had to say something. To my surprise, I began to tell a story.

One day in a remote village there was a farmer who discovered that his horse ran away. All the villagers came to him and said, "You must be so sad that your one and only horse ran away." The farmer responded strangely with just one word, "Maybe." The next day his horse returned with nine other horses. All the villagers approached him and said, "You must be so happy because not only did you get your horse back, but now you have ten instead of one." The farmer once again responded in a strange manner with just one word, "Maybe." The following day the farmer's son was out breaking in one of the new wild colts and was violently bucked off and broke his leg. All the villagers came and exclaimed, "You must be so sad that your son broke his leg." The farmer responded once again with the word, "Maybe." The next morning came and the Imperial army arrived in that small village and drafted all the able-bodied young men except for the farmer's son who just broke his leg. All the villagers came to the farmer and said, "You must be so relieved that your son was not drafted by the Imperial army." The farmer simply said, "Maybe."

The moral of the story is that sometimes in life that which we think was good for us can turn out not to be and that which we think was bad for us can actually be good. In my case, I am so glad now that I lost that US Senate race even though it hurt terribly. Upon losing, Sheridan.Church exploded in growth. I was then tasked with leading an organization called Pastors For Trump, which was geared to mobilize the evangelical voting bloc for the 2024 election. This came about because I ran for office and developed a relationship with the Trump family and associates.

Upon Donald Trump becoming the 47th President, I was privileged to be in the Oval Office on February 7, 2025, when the President signed the Executive Order establishing the new White House Faith Office in the West Wing. I was also privileged to have dinner at the White House for Easter 2025 with President Trump and a few other Pastors & Ministry Leaders such as Paula White, Franklin Graham, Kenneth Copeland and Jentzen Franklin.

It was through a painful loss that I discovered purpose in my life as a Pastor who has been given access to influence American politics. Rejection is often God's direction in disguise. The reason I choose to be involved politically is because politics directly impacts policy and policy directly impacts people. As a Pastor, I want people to be blessed, and God opened a door for me to have influence through a painful time in my life. Pain is inevitable. Instead of just going through the pain, choose to grow in the middle of it. God can help you discover your purpose even when life hurts. Finding purpose brings both happiness and holiness into our lives.

"I heard a loud voice from the throne saying, 'Look! God's dwelling place is now among the people, and he will dwell with them. They will be his people, and God himself will be with them and be their God. 4 'He will wipe every tear from their eyes. There will be no more death' or mourning or crying or pain, for the old order of things has passed away.'"
– Revelation 21:3-4

[11] Interesting note, John authored the Book of Revelation while in Exile on the island of Patmos. John was arrested and made to stand before the Emperor Domitian (93 AD). John refused to worship Domitian and he refused to confess that Caesar was Lord. In a fit of rage, Domitian demanded that John was to be thrown in a vat of boiling oil. To the surprise of everyone, John was unharmed. Since Domitian could not kill the last living Apostle, he had John exiled as a political prisoner to live out the rest of his days on the island of Patmos. This exile was no small matter because Patmos was nothing but rocks and had no vegetation. Other than rocks, Patmos was full of criminals and/ or political enemies of the Emperor. Yet, in the midst of these dire conditions John received his greatest revelation.

HOW TO CATCH THE WIND

CHAPTER 3

"Draw near to God and He will come near to you"
– James 4:8

Go back in time with me to around the year 30 AD in a small area of the vast Roman Empire called Judea. There a young Rabbi from Nazareth delivered His first and most famous sermon overlooking the majestic Sea of Galilee. We now refer to this message as the "Sermon on the Mount." It is the manifesto of Christ Jesus to His followers for this age. The Gospel of Luke gives us the *Reader's Digest* version of the sermon, while Matthew's account gives us 111 verses (3 chapters) of a radically new and counter-cultural way of thinking and living. This sermon is the King making a Kingdom announcement to His subjects on how we are to live and operate within His Kingdom.

> **"Now when Jesus saw the crowds, he went up on a mountainside and sat down. His disciples came to him, [2] and he began to teach them."**
>
> – Matthew 5:1-2

The ministry of Jesus while He was here on planet earth nearly 2,000 years ago was three-fold: **"Jesus went throughout Galilee, teaching in their synagogues, proclaiming the good news of the kingdom, and healing every disease and sickness among the people"** (Matthew 4:23).

The three-fold ministry of Jesus was *preaching, teaching and healing.*

- **Preaching** is to proclaim God's Word.
- **Teaching** is to explain God's Word.
- **Healing** is to demonstrate God's Word.

All three components are necessary to comprise the full Gospel. However, I believe the American Church has been preached to death. There is a great need currently for in-depth Gospel teaching. I learned a hard, yet valuable, lesson when I first began pastoring.

One Sunday, I preached a message about forgiveness, and I preached it very well by the way... I shouted when I needed to shout, and I whispered when I needed to whisper to help nudge the congregation to realize that they must forgive people who have hurt and wronged them. After the service, a dear brother approached me and said "That was the best sermon I have ever heard on forgiveness. In fact, it made me realize who I need to forgive. But pastor, you did not tell me how to forgive." Those words pierced my heart. I preached and proclaimed "FORGIVE! FORGIVE! FORGIVE!" But to my failure and to the disservice of my audience, I never explained how to forgive. With just the proclamation of the need to forgive, but not the explanation or demonstration of how to forgive, it brought about frustration to my listeners. In this book, I could emphasize over and over: BE

HAPPY! BE HAPPY! BE HAPPY! I might even convince you of the absolute necessity of being happy so you can be holy, but if we were honest, none of us really know how to be happy which is why we try so many different things.

Thankfully, 2,000 years ago, Jesus sat down and taught us through the "Sermon on the Mount." It is here that He presented the step-by-step guide of how to be happy. The introduction to the "Sermon on the Mount" is the step-by-step guide on happiness.

"Blessed are the poor in spirit, for theirs is the kingdom of heaven. ⁴ Blessed are those who mourn, for they will be comforted. ⁵ Blessed are the meek, for they will inherit the earth. 6 Blessed are those who hunger and thirst for righteousness, for they will be filled. ⁷ Blessed are the merciful, for they will be shown mercy. ⁸ Blessed are the pure in heart, for they will see God. ⁹ Blessed are the peacemakers, for they will be called children of God. ¹⁰ Blessed are those who are persecuted because of righteousness, for theirs is the kingdom of heaven. ¹¹ "Blessed are you when people insult you, persecute you and falsely say all kinds of evil against you because of me. ¹² Rejoice and be glad, because great is your reward in heaven, for in the same way they persecuted the prophets who were before you."
– Matthew 5:3-12

This section is called the "Beatitudes." The word "Beatitude" comes from the Latin word beatus which is where we get the English word *blessed*. Blessed literally means *"Oh how happy."* Every time that Jesus said, "Blessed are the _____", He was saying "Oh how happy are the ____". It is interesting because surveys are done asking people what they believe will make them happy. The answers range from good health to vast wealth, or from experiencing great humor to finding the love of one's life. Jesus, however, said something that none of the surveys say about what brings true and lasting happiness.

In the Old Testament, we are given Ten Commandments through Moses of instructions what not to do in order to be holy. In the New Testament, we are given Eight Beatitudes through Jesus of guidance what to do in order to be happy.

Beatitude #1 – Poor In Spirit. Oh how happy are those who are poor in spirit. Talk about a confusing opening line. So, what was Jesus saying? Poor in spirit has nothing to do with financial poverty but instead spiritual poverty. When someone is financially in poverty, they become dependent upon others to meet their needs because they do not have the means or ability to do so. When someone is rich financially, they operate very independently because they can take care of themselves. Spiritual poverty is recognizing that apart from God, we can do nothing. In our current wretched state, we are totally dependent upon God. The very first issue that Jesus addressed in the first line of His first public sermon is the issue of **PRIDE**. (We will come back to this).

Beatitude #2 – Those Who Mourn. Oh how happy are those who mourn. Once again this does not make a ton of sense. There is a possible two-fold aspect to this. First, when we grieve over suffering there is the promise of comfort. As we saw in the previous chapter, God knows how to bring about happiness even in hard times. Secondly, when we realize that we are spiritually poor, it should cause us to mourn over our seemingly hopeless state, but we are not left without hope.

Beatitude #3 – The Meek. Oh how happy are the meek. To be meek does not mean to be weak. For Jesus was the meekest man to ever live but was definitely not the weakest. Meekness is power under control. Think of the imagery of a wild horse being broken for a purpose. To be meek is to be like a domesticated animal. It amazes me how a powerful 900-pound horse can be controlled by a young girl weighing less than 90 pounds. A broken horse is a meek horse, and therefore, a useful one.

Beatitude #4 – Hunger & Thirst For Righteousness. Oh how happy are those who hunger and thirst for righteousness. When we reach a place of desiring the things of God, we will find ourselves being filled with the joy, peace, and love that God can only provide.

Beatitude #5 – The Merciful. Oh how happy are the merciful. We are told to seek justice but to love mercy (Micah 6:8). We are also informed that the amount of mercy we extend others is the amount of mercy that will be extended to us. There comes a real joy in extending mercy and forgiveness.

Beatitude #6 – Pure In Heart. Oh how happy are the pure in heart. It is awfully miserable wearing a mask in life and trying to fake it until you make it. Ask me how I know that one. I have discovered that God will not bless the pretend you, but only the real you. The authentic you, not the Instagram you. We live in a world full of filters and a byproduct of the filters we live behind is unhappiness because we are constantly comparing our fake filters with other fake filters. Comparison robs us of our joy and peace.

Beatitude #7 – The Peacemakers. Oh how happy are the peacemakers. In a world full of strife and division, peacemakers are a breeze of fresh air on a cruel hot day. It is hard to be happy when you are living with strife towards another person. There is an age-old dilemma: would you rather be right or would you rather be good? Sometimes, you cannot be both simultaneously. Ask any married couple and they will verify this. There are times in relationships that you might be right but you need to choose to be good so that there is peace rather than strife. Where there is strife there is pride (Proverbs 13:10), but love covers a multitude of sins (1 Peter 4:8).

Beatitude #8 – The Persecuted. Oh how happy are the persecuted. Most people would not say that they find happiness in being persecuted. But maybe, Jesus knew something that we do not just yet.

STEPS 1-8

To bring all of this together, we must first understand the progression of the eight Beatitudes. Jesus began with the need for us to recognize our spiritual poverty. Without God, we are wretched. This realization should cause us to mourn over our spiritual state of being. The genuine mourning over our spiritual condition will then produce a meekness and a humility that otherwise would never develop naturally. The first three Beatitudes are all about emptying yourself of *yourself*. When you are so full of you, it is hard to be filled with the things of God such as joy, peace, and love.

Upon emptying yourself of yourself, there will be a void and something or someone will have to fill the vacancy. Your soul will become hungry and thirsty. The reason so many people do not hunger and thirst after righteousness is because they are completely full of themselves and the things this life offers. But when we get hungry and thirsty, we are promised that we will be filled with God's righteousness, which will then begin to manifest certain behaviors. When God's righteousness fills us, ONLY then can we be merciful, just as God is merciful. We can be pure, just as God is pure. We can be peacemakers, just as God is the ultimate peacemaker. This is the method by which we become like Christ.

Once we start acting as Christ acted, we will then be treated as Christ was treated. The world persecutes that which is different. The great Philosopher, Socrates was executed for being different. Why was the co-founder of Western Civilization put to death? He denied polytheism and embraced monotheism. Because Socrates was different, he was persecuted. As followers of Jesus, we are to be radically different. We are to march to the sound of a different beat than the world around us. We are called to be different so that we can make a difference. By being different, we will be persecuted. In fact, Jesus made us a promise. He told his disciples, **"In this world you will have trouble. But take heart! I have overcome the world"** (John 16:33). If we follow Jesus and model His life in our own life, then we will experience trouble. But Jesus encouraged us to take heart (be of good cheer, be happy) because He has overcome the very world that persecuted Him and will persecute us. This tells me that true happiness is not circumstantial and subjective, but rather an objective state of being in Christ. **Happiness is not the absence of problems in our life, but happiness is the presence of Christ in our life.** The indication of God's presence is joy (Psalm 16:11).

FIRST THINGS FIRST

How can we achieve this objective state of being happy even while being persecuted? We must put first things first. The first step to true happiness is putting to death our own pride, ego, and independence. Jesus began His sermon with the greatest battle we all face, ourselves. It is interesting that in the first sermon of Jesus, His very first issue He chose to deal with was pride. That is because pride is our greatest enemy. It is a spiritual cancer that promises happiness but only produces misery. Pride is an independent attitude. Pride leaves God out of the picture. Augustine, Luther, Calvin, and Lewis all agreed that pride is the greatest sin of them all. **Pride turned glorious angels into miserable devils, but humility turns wretched sinners into happy and holy saints.** God opposes the proud, but He gives grace to the humble (James 4:6). The reason people who are prideful are truly miserable is because God Himself is against them. The reason truly humble people are genuinely happy is because the happiest Being of all (God) is for them.

How do we experience the death of pride? This is a necessary process in the life of a believer. Before God ever does anything great through us, He must first do something great in us. I want to briefly tell the story of three incredible men in the Old Testament that God used greatly but first had to have their egos checked: Moses, David, and Elijah. These three men also represent the three offices in ancient Israel: Priest, King, and Prophet.

MOSES

Let's begin with looking at the most highly revered figure in Judaism, Moses. Interesting fact, Moses is the only person in the Old Testament who functioned in all three Old Testament offices simultaneously. Moses served as Prophet, Priest, and Judge (precursor to King) for Israel on behalf of God. The life of Moses can be broken down into three parts. D.L. Moody said that, "Moses spent his first forty years thinking he was somebody. He spent his next forty years learning he was a nobody. And he spent his third forty years discovering what God can do with a nobody." God specializes in taking ordinary people and using them for extraordinary purposes. Moses is a prime example of that. One of the lessons we learn from the life of Moses is that in answering the call of God, timing is crucial. Early on in Moses' life he tried rushing his calling; he tried speeding things up. He got a little anxious like many of us.

Moses was born at a time when the Hebrew people were slaves in captivity in Egypt. At that time, Pharaoh was pressing the Hebrew people extremely hard, yet they kept having so many babies that he was afraid they would rise up and be a threat to his Empire. Pharaoh sent out a decree that all boys born of the Hebrews were to be put to death at birth. This probably sounds familiar to you in regard to the birth of Jesus. That is because Moses was a type[13] of Christ. **Deuteronomy 18:15 & 18 says, "The Lord your God will raise up for you a prophet like me (Moses) from among you, from your fellow Israelites. You must listen to him… I will raise up for them a prophet like you from among their fellow Israelites, and I will put my words in his mouth. He will tell them everything I command him."**

[12] Dwight Lyman Moody was an American evangelist who founded the Moody Church, Moody Bible Institute and Moody Publishers

Moses and Jesus were both born under ruthless rulers (Pharoah & Herod) that gave a genocidal order to kill the Hebrew boys, but both Moses and Jesus survived. Jesus and Moses left Royalty and entered obscurity to accomplish their mission. The first public miracle of Moses was turning water into blood while the first public miracle of Jesus was turning water into wine. Both Moses and Jesus were rejected at their first appearance by the Hebrew people. Moses was received at his second appearance, and we are told at the Second Coming of Christ, the Jewish people will receive Him as Messiah. There are many more of these examples, but this is enough to see that Moses was a foreshadowing of the coming Christ.

"At that time Moses was born, and he was no ordinary child. For three months he was cared for by his family.[21] When he was placed outside, Pharaoh's daughter took him and brought him up as her own son. [22] Moses was educated in all the wisdom of the Egyptians and was powerful in speech and action. [23] "When Moses was forty years old, he decided to visit his own people, the Israelites. [24] He saw one of them being mistreated by an Egyptian, so he went to his defense and avenged him by killing the Egyptian. [25] Moses thought that his own people would realize that God was using him to rescue them, but they did not. [26] The next day Moses came upon two Israelites who were fighting. He tried to reconcile them by saying, 'Men, you are brothers; why do you want to

[12] Typology is the study of how God used events, people, and institutions in the Old Testament to foreshadow events, people, and institutions in the New Testament, ultimately pointing to Jesus Christ.

hurt each other?' ²⁷ "But the man who was mistreating the other pushed Moses aside and said, 'Who made you ruler and judge over us? ²⁸ Are you thinking of killing me as you killed the Egyptian yesterday?' ²⁹ When Moses heard this, he fled to Midian, where he settled as a foreigner and had two sons."

- Acts 7:20-29

The three verses I underlined above are the summary of the first forty years of Moses' life. Moses was called by God to be the deliverer for the Hebrew people. He was trained in all the wisdom of Egypt, which at that time was the most sophisticated society in the ancient near east. Moses would have attended what was called the Temple of the Sun in Egypt. It was the Harvard of the ancient world. It was there that he was trained in different types of languages, skills, and military strategies. Moses was being prepared for the throne of Egypt. Historians tell us that the Pharaoh at this time did not have a son, and that Moses was being groomed to be a future Pharaoh.

The Book of Acts also informs us that Moses was mighty in both word and deed. Which means he was a person of great charisma and accomplishment. Moses had it all going for him. He had the highest levels of education one could have. He was a military leader before he was forty. He had great charisma and was being trained for power in Egypt. However, Moses knew that God had a call on his life. Moses was not supposed to be a Pharaoh, but he was supposed to deliver God's people from the chains of Pharaoh.

Although Moses knew the will and call of God for his life by the age of forty, he did not know the timing of God. So, he tried to force the will of God with his own plan, his own strength, and his own ability and arrogance. One hot day in Egypt, Moses came to the defense of a Hebrew who was being beaten and Moses killed the Egyptian taskmaster in the process. Moses buried him in the sand and thought this act would start the Exodus that God had called him to lead.

Unfortunately, this was neither God's way nor His timing. What is interesting is the way that **Exodus 2:12** describes what happened: "**Looking this way and that and seeing no one, he killed the Egyptian and hid him in the sand.**" Moses knew it was God's will that he would deliver the Hebrew people and he gets an idea that now is the time. What did Moses do? He looked to his left and then he looked to his right. But Moses never looked up. He did not involve God in the equation. Out of pride and independence, Moses launched a premature strike, which resulted in a forty-year setback. The lesson here is that our pride will shout to us that we are ready prematurely, while God will whisper to us "just be steady for I am still getting you ready."

Every season in our lives is significant and we can enjoy every season that we are in even if it is a season of preparation. I learned something very interesting when my wife, Kendra, was pregnant with our youngest daughter, Eva.

One day Kendra thought she was having some complications with the pregnancy, so we went to the Hospital just to be safe. When we arrived, Kendra was having consistent contractions which we thought meant that Eva might be trying to come early.

We were praying that was not the case. I learned that sometimes the baby can try to come early, but if the doctors catch it quick enough, they can give a certain medication that will delay the birth. They know it is best for the baby to stay the full term rather than be born prematurely. Although the baby may really want to come early, what is best for them is to stay the entire time. If Eva had been delivered that day, it would have been a setback for her right out of the gate. She would have had to stay in the NICU (Neonatal Intensive Care Unit) and would have to be constantly monitored.

Sometimes, we are like those babies who want to come early. We think we are ready, but God, like an experienced obstetrician (OB), knows it is best for us to stay in our incubation process just a little longer. If you rush things like Moses did out of pride, you too could experience a forty-year setback and end up in a desert. May we learn from Moses' mistake that even if we know the will of God for our lives, we still need to seek God's timing and remain totally dependent on Him.

But maybe you are like me and you have rushed things. I know there are times I have forced things that I knew was God's will, but I learned the hard way that it was not God's timing. We can learn from those mistakes made out of pride. We can learn from the failures of rushing in too soon. Sometimes failure is a better teacher than success ever could be. Former heavy-weight boxer James "Quick" Tillis, who fought out in Chicago in the early 1980's, tells the story of his first day in the Windy City after arriving from his hometown of Tulsa, OK. "I got off the bus with two suitcases under my arms in downtown Chicago and stopped in front of the Sears Tower. I put my suitcases down, and I looked up at the Tower and I said to myself, 'I'm going to conquer Chicago.' "When I looked down, the suitcases were gone." Pride goes before the fall (Proverbs 16:18).

The good news is that with God, failure is never final. Failure is just an opportunity to start again with much greater understanding. Moses failed in Egypt and God used it as an opportunity to teach him humility. At the age of forty, Moses had all the education and experience that he needed to be the deliverer of the Hebrew people except one important ingredient: **HUMILITY**.

Moses relied on his strength and abilities instead of God. But through his failure he would gain humility. Scripture says, "Moses was the most humble person to ever live" (See Numbers 12:13). Humility is often learned through failure rather than success. Moses had to flee as the Prince of Egypt and he ended up as a lowly Shepherd in the desert. Talk about eating some humble pie. Here is the man of God with the call of God. He had the training and the giftings. He was powerful in word and deed. But he became a fugitive on the run hiding in the desert with sheep.

Moses found himself at the prime age of forty as a nomad in the desert. He was a foreigner living in a foreign land and in fact he was in this desert for the next forty years of his life. He entered what Charles Swindoll[14] describes as "God's University of the Desert." God has a university that every one of His people who will answer His call must graduate from.

I remember when I graduated from High School in Oklahoma and was preparing to attend Oral Roberts University. It was exciting and yet very nerve-wracking. It was a new world for me at 18 years old. On my first day, I remember walking up from the parking lot and there was a group of upperclassmen all dressed up in blue and gold with pom-poms cheering for all the freshmen on their first day and welcoming us to the new community. On that day, I met several people I am still friends with today. I had a great time at ORU and loved every second of it, so much so, that I stayed at ORU to earn my M.A. in Theological & Historical Studies.

[14] Charles Swindoll is the Founding Pastor at Stonebriar Community Church, in Frisco, Texas and served as President of Dallas Theological Seminary. Christianity Today named Swindoll as one of the top 25 most influential preachers of the past 50 years.

Unfortunately, God's University is nothing like the college that you or I attended. It is very, very different. It is a lonely campus with just me, myself, and I. There is no welcoming party, there are no pom-poms, there are no basketball or football games. It feels like a wasteland. And the tuition is quite costly.

Contrary to popular belief there is a cost to following Jesus. Sadly, today it comes across too many that if you become a Christian then God will suddenly wave a magic wand over your life and make you happy, healthy, wealthy, and wise with no cost. Many believe if you become a Christian, God will give you everything yet require nothing from you so you can live happily ever after. This is not the Gospel that has been passed down from generation to generation beginning with the Apostles. That is a distorted "gospel" isolated primarily to 20th and 21st Century American Christianity. There is a cost to following Jesus, but it is well worth the cost, let me assure you of that.

At God's University of Humility, He takes ordinary people like you and me who are full of ourselves, and He empties us and transforms us into extraordinary people who He can use to bring about His plan and His purpose. It might take some of us four years to graduate, while others, like Moses, may need forty years to graduate. But this University of Humility is designed to prepare each of us to be happy and holy.

Moses found himself in the middle of nowhere as a Shepherd working for his father-in-law, Jethro. Think about it for a moment: Moses was highly educated and experienced but found himself living in the desert watching sheep that were not even his. The Prince of Egypt became nothing more than a Shepherd of a handful of sheep. This was a job that most people would have looked down upon, especially Egyptians. **"For all shepherds are detestable to the Egyptians"** (Genesis 46:34). Moses spent his first forty years of life thinking he was a somebody. He had the call of God, the education, the experience, the background, and the giftings. He soon realized he was just a nobody on the backside of the desert. He went from being a celebrity in Egypt to an unknown in Midian. That must have crushed the ego of this once great and proud leader. What Moses did not know was that he was being trained in the desert to lead God's people to the Promised Land through this same desert.

Moses spent forty years in the desert. These were his so-called prime years of life. From the age of forty to eighty. He did not graduate from God's University of Humility until he was eighty years old. That is a long time. There was nothing comfortable about those forty years in the desert. When we are uncomfortable that we are being stretched, we grow the most. Moses was accustomed to the royal lifestyle in Egypt living off the Nile River in the Palace of Pharaoh. Moses had everything handed to him since Pharaoh's daughter drew him out of the water. Now nothing was being handed to him. It was rough. He was learning humility. This is challenging for all of us. Not everyone will choose to go through the courses on Humility because the price is so high. But the reward is well worth it. When Moses graduated from the forty-year test there was a burning bush awaiting him.

One day Moses was minding his own business, when he saw a bush that was on fire but was not burning up. Out of that bush he heard the audible voice of God speak and he heard God say it was time to go and deliver the people of Israel. Finally, it was time for his destiny to be fulfilled. Unlike forty years prior, Moses was a broken man but he was given a second chance by God. Exodus 3:4 says, **"When the Lord saw that he had gone over to look, God called to him from within the bush, "Moses! Moses!" And Moses said, "Here I am."** Forty years earlier Moses would have tried to impress God with his list of accomplishments. But now Moses was a humbled man. He simply responded to the voice of God by saying, "Here I am." God is not impressed by the resume of accomplishments we have saved on Google Docs, or on our computer somewhere. God is looking for a heart of humility.

Moses passed the test and would go on to lead God's people out of the bondages of Egypt and became one of the greatest vessels to ever be used by God. This strong, passionate and prideful man was turned into a meek and humble man that was truly used by God. We have the same invitation as well but we have to stay in the process of God developing us like He did with Moses.

ELIJAH

We now examine the most respected and revered prophet of ancient Israel, Elijah. The life and ministry of Elijah can be summarized in one word… crazy. It is truly remarkable. Some of us have lived a life full of wild experiences and events. Great tragedies and great victories. All of those things, the wins and the losses, the pain and joy, all go into making who we are. Elijah's life is one of an extreme rollercoaster ride. One minute he is up on top of the mountain and the next he is down at the bottom of the valley. But through it all God molded and shaped him to be the legendary prophet who we are still talking about today.

There is a story I want to share that I think represents the life of Elijah. The story goes like this: Once, an extremely eccentric and wealthy man threw a party at his mansion with all of his rich friends. In his backyard, he had just installed a massive pool filled with sharks and alligators. On the night of the party, the wealthy man announced to everyone that he would give a person anything they wanted and it did not matter how much it cost if someone would jump into the pool and swim to the other side. A few moments later there was a splash in the pool. Everyone looked and there was a man swimming for his life - dodging sharks, and alligators. Finally, with many close calls, the man jumped out of the pool in a frenzy. When he got out, he looked scared to death and was trying to catch his breath. The wealthy man was amazed. He said, "Sir, you are the bravest person I have ever met. I will give you anything you want, just name it. What do you want?" The man, still trying to catch his breath said, "I want the name of the person who pushed me in!" That right there is the story of Elijah's life in a nutshell.

In Israel at that time there were all these sharks and alligators that invaded God's pool. Elijah got pushed into this pool and swam frantically for his life dodging sharks and alligators one after another. When he finally reached the other side of the pool he said, "Who shoved me into that pool?" God said, "I did." But God did it for a reason. He was developing Elijah into a man of greatness. He was developing a legend of the faith. Maybe you feel like your life has been one of constantly dodging sharks and alligators in a pool that you got pushed into like Elijah. Take heart because **the God who puts us in the pool is the God who is with us in the pool** as Elijah discovered.

1st Kings 17 is where the story of Elijah begins, but for there to be a hero there must be a villain. There were plenty of villains in Israel at the time. Quick history lesson to help give a little context of what was taking place in 1st Kings 17. When King Solomon, the son of David and the wisest man to ever live, died, the nation of Israel split in two and became two very different nations. After 931 BC, the northern nation was called Israel, and the southern nation was called Judah. The southern Kingdom, Judah, did ok for a while, they had some good kings and they had some bad kings. The north on the other hand, was a totally different story. They went through a period of having nineteen straight evil kings. Think about that for a moment. Here in the United States, we may get a wicked president here or there (although we have had many incompetent ones) but imagine nineteen straight evil presidents in a row. There would be a lot of sharks and alligators in our cultural pool. But that is exactly what happened in the northern kingdom. After nineteen straight evil kings there came another king named Ahab. Ahab is described as the most wicked king of them all. What a title to hold. Out of nineteen straight evil kings, Ahab was the worst.

Ahab's not-so-better half was his wife, Jezebel. She was the real power. Ahab might have been the "head" but Jezebel was definitely the "neck." As one man said, "She may have been Ahab's wife, but she was the Devil's woman for the hour." Jezebel flooded Israel with the worship of Baal and brought in the prophets of Asherah. Baal and Asherah worship consisted of child sacrifice to the gods, as well as cultic prostitution. Essentially the religion worked like this: the people would sacrifice children to please their gods, they also would go have sex with temple prostitutes as acts of worship. Both of these acts were and still are an abomination to the God of Abraham, Isaac, and Jacob. To make matters even worse, the false prophets were put on the state payroll, thanks to Jezebel. All of this was going on in God's pool - God's nation.

After nineteen straight evil kings God finally said, "enough is enough." The corruption, wickedness and evil had to be dealt with. God decided it was time to clean up the pool and Elijah was the man that God selected for the task.

"Now Elijah the Tishbite, from Tishbe in Gilead, said to Ahab, "As the Lord, the God of Israel, lives, whom I serve, there will be neither dew nor rain in the next few years except at my word."

- 1st Kings 17:1

Wow, what an introduction. There are a few things that stand out about Elijah in this opening verse. Elijah's name comes from three different Hebrew root words, which when combined together mean, "The Lord is my God." Baal might be the god of Ahab and Jezebel but the Lord is Elijah's God. Next, he is identified as Elijah the Tishbite. It's like saying Jackson Lahmeyer from Tulsa, Oklahoma. The place where Elijah was from was a very small and remote place. It was insignificant. But out of this insignificant place God would train up a legend to do significant things. Elijah entered the scene like a wrecking ball. He got right up in the wicked king's face and declared a major drought was coming as God's judgement.

Elijah served as God's prophet. He called forth a drought and this was a big deal. For Israel at that time, it was not just an economic recession like that of 2008 in America, but it was a complete economic depression, far worse than the Great Depression of 1929. The entire Israelite economy was built on agriculture. With no rain for several years, the sector of agriculture does not do too well. God's hand of punishment was clearly evident. Elijah confronted the evil king with the courage of a bold lion; you would think after this great victory God would have had Elijah continue and fight to win more victories against corruption. But God's ways are not always our ways. Instead of telling Elijah to stay and fight Ahab, God told Elijah to go and hide.

"Then the word of the Lord came to Elijah: ³ "Leave here, turn eastward and hide in the Kerith Ravine, east of the Jordan."

- 1st Kings 17:2-3

The Kerith Ravine for Elijah was equivalent to the University of Humility for Moses in the desert. Elijah entered the scene and immediately confronted the king with boldness - but afterward, God told him to go and hide. I imagine Elijah thinking to himself, "Go and hide? I want to stay and fight. I'm a lion-hearted prophet." And God gently whispered back, "You are right, but you are not ready just yet. There are still some things I need to do inside of you so I can do even greater things through you." God told Elijah that he needed to enter a season of preparation. Just like with Moses, before God can really use someone, He has to first prepare them. That preparation for Elijah would take place at the Kerith Ravine.

The word Kerith means to *cut off or to cut down*. At the Kerith Ravine which was located East of the Jordan, Elijah got cut down. It was here that God cut him down in order to build him back up. When Elijah first appeared, he was God's spokesperson and was identified by his hometown. He was Elijah the Tishbite. After Kerith, he will be identified not by his hometown but instead as "Elijah a man of God" for the rest of the Bible. It is at the Kerith Ravine that we are developed into a man or a woman of God.

Elijah started in the spotlight; he was at the palace of the king but at Kerith he was in absolute anonymity. Being in the shadows can hurt sometimes because we do not receive the attention, we feel that we deserve. AW Tozer[15] once said, "It is doubtful that God can bless a man greatly until He has hurt him deeply." Being cut down is painful. But the greater the hurt the greater the usefulness; the greater the pain you have experienced the greater God can use you. The more God breaks you the greater He can use you. Elijah was humbled privately at the Kerith Ravine so God could use him publicly.

Aiden Wilson Tozer was an American pastor who authored many well-known books such as *"The Pursuit of God."*

We often think to ourselves that God would never want to cut me down or change who I am. There is the famous, yet not-so-accurate saying, "God loves me just the way I am…" That is beyond false. God does not love us just the way we are. God loves us so much more than that. In fact, He does not allow us to stay the way we are, but He changes us out of His great love for us.

A story that has stuck with me which is a little gross but has a great lesson goes like this: There was a happy little bird who was flying south for the winter. Unfortunately, that little bird got caught in a blizzard and the ice started sticking to its wings and all of a sudden, the bird's wings got frozen. The bird thought to itself, "I am going to die now." As the bird crashed on the ground it landed underneath a cow. Well, that cow dumped a load of… yes, manure on that little bird. The bird could not believe that the cow did that to him. The bird said, "Unbelievable, I cannot believe I am going to die like this." But the heat from the manure actually melted the ice off the little bird and he was now safe from the frigid weather conditions. However, there came a cat. The cat decided to rescue the little bird out of the manure. When the cat pulled the bird out of the manure the cat actually ate the bird, and the bird died.

Ok, here is the moral of the story: not everyone who dumps on you in life is against you and not everyone who helps pull you up is for you. Elijah must have felt like he had been dumped on by God. But it was for his good. When God sends us to the Kerith Ravine it is to teach us total dependency on Him. In other words, pride must be killed so that humility can be birthed.

"You will drink from the brook, and I have directed the ravens to supply you with food there." ⁵ So he did what the Lord had told him. He went to the Kerith Ravine, east of the Jordan, and stayed there. ⁶ The ravens brought him bread and meat in the morning and bread and meat in the evening, and he drank from the brook."

- 1st Kings 17:4-6

God guided Elijah to the Kerith Ravine, where he was cut down in hiding, but God promised to provide for Elijah while he was there. It was not the normal means of provision either. Ravens brought Elijah meat and bread every morning and evening. The original *Doordash*. Ravens brought Elijah everyday Chick-fil-a (God's favorite restaurant) at 9 am and at 5 pm. Notice that the Ravens did not bring seven breakfast sandwiches and seven chicken sandwiches on Monday so there was enough food for the entire week. No, they brought one Chick-fil-a sandwich at 9 am and one at 5 pm and that was it. Just enough for that day and that day only. Now imagine this every single day for months or even years during the drought. No doubt that Elijah wondered, "What if the Raven does not come today?" Elijah was learning to be totally dependent upon God.

At Kerith we all learn how to trust God day by day. God did not give a three-month supply, only enough for that day. God was teaching Elijah trust. There are seasons in life where God will not give us more than what we need, but just exactly what we need for that day. He did this with the Hebrew people when they left Egypt. Out in the desert God fed them supernaturally with Manna falling from heaven. God told them to only collect enough food for each day. If they collected food for tomorrow, just in case the Manna did not fall, it would go bad and be rotten. Why did God tell the people of Israel in the desert only to collect enough for the day? He was teaching them how to depend on Him day by day. How to be people of genuine faith. When Jesus taught his disciples to pray, He said pray like this, "Give us this day our daily bread." He did not say to pray about getting bread for tomorrow. He said pray for this day our daily bread. Enough for today. God wants each of us to learn to be totally dependent upon Him every single day.

It is at the Kerith Ravine we learn not to worry about tomorrow, but to trust God for today. God will provide for you; it may not be more than enough at times but it will be just enough. Through the Kerith Ravine experience, we will come out not as Elijah the Tishbite, but as Elijah the man of God. I do not want to be just Jackson Lahmeyer of Tulsa, Oklahoma; I want to be Jackson Lahmeyer the man of God. That is my prayer for you as well. A man or a woman of God is dependent upon God day by day. Trust God for today.

DAVID

One of the great things about the Bible is that the stories of our heroes are not cookie-cutter fairy tales. Instead, they are real, raw and totally relatable to the lives we live every day. Stories are powerful teaching tools because they translate truth to us that we better understand. The stories of the Bible help strengthen us as we go through the same experiences that many of our favorite biblical characters went through. Did you know that more is written about King David than any other Old Testament character? Abraham has fourteen chapters written about him and so does Joseph. David has around sixty-six chapters written about his life and that does not include the fifty-nine times he is mentioned in the New Testament.

On the surface, however, there seemed to be nothing about David that would have impressed God, or you and I. David was much like the other Hebrew boys of his day. There was nothing too unique about his outward appearance that made one pause and say "hmm..." He was nothing more than a young Shepherd of a few sheep from a little village called Bethlehem. Yet, God looked beyond all of that and saw who David was on the inside. God began the work of developing humility in David at a young age.

On two different occasions David was referred to as a man after God's own heart. However, David was a nobody to begin with. Sometimes people will ask, "What was inside David that was so special? What was it that made David a man after God's own heart?" There are a few key ingredients that, I believe, made David a man after God's heart. Those include faith, humility, loyalty, and integrity. Too often people look at the outward appearance, but thankfully God looks at the heart. In fact, the prophet Samuel fell for this trap when he went to anoint one of the sons of Jesse as the new king. Jesse brought out all of his sons except one and Samuel looked at them starting with the oldest.

"When they arrived, Samuel saw Eliab and thought, "Surely the Lord's anointed stands here before the Lord." ⁷ But the Lord said to Samuel, "Do not consider his appearance or his height, for I have rejected him. The Lord does not look at the things people look at. People look at the outward appearance, but the Lord looks at the heart."

- 1st Samuel 16:6

Samuel was caught looking at the appearance of David's older brother. God corrected him, and Samuel proceeded to ask Jesse if he had any other sons. Jesse responded by saying, "Yes, he is with the sheep." When Samuel saw David, God said to him this is the new King of Israel and Samuel went on to anoint him. David was selected to be king by God because he was a man after God's heart. Now remember, some of those invisible qualities that made David a man after God's heart: faith, humility, loyalty, and integrity. Where did these qualities develop in him? David spent day after day, night after night alone in the fields with just his sheep and with God. It was there that he was being prepared to be the King. Like Moses in the desert and Elijah at the Kerith Ravine, David was prepared for the limelight in the field of the shadows. Moses, Elijah and David were all humbled privately so God could use them publicly. David was trained in the shepherd's field to be ready to take over the King's palace. God taught David humility privately so that He could exalt him publicly.

I can remember when I was an intern at a small country church while I was a student at Oral Roberts University in Tulsa, Oklahoma. The pastor there was in his 80's and would occasionally ask me to preach. I had never preached before and today I feel really sorry for those people who had to listen to those early sermons from an arrogant and undeveloped preacher. I am sure they will be greatly rewarded in Heaven for enduring those early messages. However, I remember this Pastor sharing with me how when I get up to minister it is so important that I minister out of humility and not pride. Now, humility is not thinking less of ourselves in terms of quality, but thinking more about God.

This wise Pastor told me a story of a young preacher who was getting ready to preach for the very first time. This young preacher was well prepared and he knew he was well prepared. He walked up on stage with his head held high and chest puffed out. He grabbed the microphone, and he froze. Nothing came out of his mouth. All the hours of study and nothing. He put the mic down and walked off stage with his head towards the ground and an older preacher leaned over to console him and said, "if you would have walked up there the way you walked down then God could have used you." I will never forget that, and it has stuck with me ever since. It has made me recognize my own need to be a person of humility.

David was a man of humility. When Samuel anointed David as the next King of Israel as a teenager, we discover something interesting about David. He did not go around bragging and boasting about it, but it says in 1st Samuel 16 that David simply went back to his sheep after being anointed king. That is quite impressive for a teenager. I mean - that is impressive for an adult as well. If most people were anointed king they would not go back and do their dull, boring, little job. In fact, they would probably refuse to go back because now they are too good for it. Most people would get on social media and blast it to the whole world: "Hey everybody! Just want to let you know that God anointed me king today!" There was none of that modern-day attitude of entitlement that is rampant in our culture with David.

Although David was anointed king, he humbly went back to his everyday life, taking care of his father's flock. What an incredible picture of humility. Because David was a man after God's heart, God began to exalt David. He began to show His favor toward David. As you know, David killed Goliath, and he became very popular in Israel. King Saul tried to kill him over the newfound popularity, but David miraculously escaped.

After David was on the run from King Saul for many years, he finally became king. From there, it was as if David's life was like an arrow soaring high in the sky. Unfortunately, sometimes the most dangerous thing for a man or woman of God is success because that is how pride can easily creep in.

As David was soaring higher and higher, his incredibly strong foundation of humility started to weaken and crack. David was successful and prospered in everything he did. David had the Midas Touch. But pride crept in. His fame increased. His wealth increased. His power increased. But so did David's ego. David had not lost a single battle as king and that great success made him comfortable which then caused him to become vulnerable.

"In the spring, at the time when kings go off to war, David sent Joab out with the king's men and the whole Israelite army. They destroyed the Ammonites and besieged Rabbah. But David remained in Jerusalem."

- 2ndSamuel 11:1

Notice that David remained in Jerusalem. David was the King of Israel. He was the one God anointed and appointed to lead Israel, yet he decided to stay home. David was not meant to stay home; he was called to lead the people in battle as the king. Remember, David had never lost a battle, he was beyond confident and comfortable. Unfortunately, he became vulnerable. He decided to kick back and relax. David's decision to stay home rather than lead in the battlefield was an act of pride.

Pride always produces disobedience, but humility produces obedience. Pride stays home in Jerusalem; humility goes out to battle. David would forever regret staying home because one evening when he should have been on the battlefield, David walked out on his balcony and saw a beautiful woman bathing; her name was Bathsheba. David said to his servants, "Guys, go get her for me." David should have never been on that balcony. He saw something he should have never seen. David should have been out on the battlefield leading his men to victory. Instead, his own pride placed him in a position of vulnerability. As you know, David and Bathsheba slept together experiencing a night of pleasure. Nothing seemed to happen that night but what David did not know was his life would soon fall apart. A period of time went by, and David got news from Bathsheba that she was pregnant. His heart sank because Bathsheba was a married woman.

It was pride that got David into the vulnerable situation, and it was pride that caused him to try and cover up his mess. Long-story short, David had Bathsheba's husband, Uriah, killed so he could cover his sin and keep it hidden from the public eye. What a disappointing and unnecessary tragedy. The man of God with a heart after God had not only committed adultery but he committed murder against an innocent man as well.

David thought like many of us so often do: "I can handle myself." I struggle in this area. My wife, Kendra, is very quick to point it out to me. She will send me on what she calls an errand; I call it a mission. It is usually to pick something up from the grocery store. One thing I am not very good at is finding things that are right in front of me. I tend to miss the obvious. Well, I will go to the store to get something and honestly, I have no clue where the item is, but rest assured I am not asking anyone for help. Every time a very nice and helpful worker will walk by and see me searching through every aisle in the store three times and will ask, "Sir, can I help you find something?" My response 100 out of 100 times after walking through the entire store three times looking for a $1 seasoning packet is, "No, I am good, I got this."

I heard a story one time about Muhammad Ali the great boxer who always rhymed things like, "Float like a butterfly, sting like a bee. The hands can't hit what the eyes can't see." Muhammad Ali was on a flight across the country and the stewardess said to him, "Sir you need to put on your seatbelt" He responded back to her that Superman (referring to himself) does not need to wear a seatbelt. She then said, "Superman does not need to be on a plane to fly either. Put your seatbelt on." David believed he did not need the seatbelt any longer. Therefore, he found himself in bed with a married woman instead of on the battlefield with his mighty men of valor.

David's life quickly became a mess, even though no one besides him and Bathsheba knew about it. However, there was someone else who knew and that was God. One day, God sends the prophet Nathan to confront King David.

"The Lord sent Nathan to David. When he came to him, he said, "There were two men in a certain town, one rich and the other poor. [2] The rich man had a very large number of sheep and cattle, [3] but the poor man had nothing except one little ewe lamb he had bought. He raised it, and it grew up with him and his children. It shared his food, drank from his cup and even slept in his arms. It was like a daughter to him. [4] "Now a traveler came to the rich man, but the rich man refrained from taking one of his own sheep or cattle to prepare a meal for the traveler who had come to him. Instead, he took the ewe lamb that belonged to the poor man and prepared it for the one who had come to him." [5] David burned with anger against the man and said to Nathan, "As surely as the Lord lives, the man who did this must die! [6] He must pay

for that lamb four times over, because he did such a thing and had no pity." ⁷ Then Nathan said to David, "You are the man!"

- 2nd Samuel 12:1

David's pride and sin was brought to his full attention. He sinned out of pride and tried covering it up. Here he had a decision to make: continue in pride or choose humility. <u>**Verse 13**</u> says, "Then **David said to Nathan, "I have sinned against the Lord."** He chose humility. After Nathan confronted David, David went on to write <u>**Psalm 51**</u> which is arguably the most beautiful Psalm other than Psalm 23. Psalm 51:1 says, **"Have mercy on me, O God, according to your unfailing love; according to your great compassion blot out my transgressions. ² Wash away all my iniquity and cleanse me from my sin. ³ For I know my transgressions, and my sin is always before me. ⁴ Against you, you only, have I sinned and done what is evil in your sight."** And in <u>**verse 10**</u> David cried out, **"Create in me a pure heart, O God, and renew a steadfast spirit within me."** Pride caused David to fall, but it was his humility that caused him to be restored. Humility sings the old hymn, "Lord, I need thee. Every hour I need thee." Humility is being totally dependent upon God. In James 4 we are told that if we sow the seed of humility, we will reap the harvest of God's grace. However, if we sow the seed of pride we will reap the opposition of God. David in that crucial moment sowed the seed of humility and reaped God's grace.

Let me try to tie this all together with one more story. There was a man who had a mansion with ten rooms. Five rooms on the first floor and five on the second. One day he heard a gentle knock at the door. He opened it up and there was Jesus, shining like the sun in all of its' brilliance. The man said "I have heard about you. You heal people, you deliver people, you provide for people, you are gracious, loving, and kind. Please come in and stay at my house." The man went on to say, "Here is what I want to do for you. I am going to give you the best room in this house which is upstairs. You will absolutely love it!"

Jesus being a gentleman accepted the offer and went upstairs to that room. Later that night the wealthy man heard a loud and horrendous knock at his door. He went to see who it was and when he cracked the door he saw the Devil. The man said, "I have heard about you. You come to steal, kill, and destroy. I do not want you in my house." He tried to close the door but the Devil had already slipped his foot in. The Devil got in his house and this man wrestled with the Devil all night long. The Devil poured temptation after temptation upon him and destroyed the whole house.

The next morning the Devil subtly slipped out the back door. Jesus came down the steps and the man said, "Lord, why did you not help me last night? Did you not hear what was happening?" Jesus said, "My friend, you only gave me one room to be in." The man said, "Oh, I see. Here is what I am going to do for you then. I am going to give you the entire upstairs. All five rooms are yours." Jesus accepted the offer and went upstairs.

Later that night there was another loud, nasty and disturbing knock at the door. Déjà vu, it was the Devil. The Devil snuck in and that man wrestled with him all night on the first floor of that house. The next morning the Devil slipped out the back door once again. Jesus came down and this time the man was angry. He said, "Jesus, I gave you half of my house and you still did absolutely nothing! Why did you allow this to happen to me?" Jesus responded, "My friend, you only gave me the upstairs." The man quickly said back, "I've got it now! Jesus you can have nine of the rooms in my house, the only one you cannot have is the one I sleep in. There are some things in there I do not really want you to see." Jesus accepted the man's offer.

Later that night there was that same nasty knock at the door. Once again it was the Devil. The Devil and that man wrestled all night in his room and by morning his room was utterly destroyed.

The next morning the man was struck with brokenness and said, "Jesus why did you not help me last night?" Jesus said, "Because you only gave me 9 rooms to live in. This house is still yours. You still have the keys. The deed is still in your name. This is your house." Suddenly the man realized that he was still operating independently. He was still the owner of the house. He swallowed his pride and decided to humble himself. He said in a sorrowful tone, "Jesus here are the keys. Here is the deed. This house is no longer mine, but it is yours." Jesus took the keys and the deed and smiled at the man and said, "Thank you my friend."

Later that night there was once again a nasty, loud knock at the door. The man began to tremble in fear for he had been down this road many times. He knew what was about to happen. As he went to answer the door, Jesus tapped on his shoulder and said, "Hold on. I will answer the door at My house." Jesus flung the door wide open and the eyes of the Devil got really big. The Devil looked at Jesus and looked at the address of the house, he looked at Jesus one more time and looked at the address of the house and said, "I apologize, I must have the wrong address." Here is the moral of the story: When we humble ourselves and give ourselves completely over to God, He will answer the door when the enemy comes knocking.

When we sow the seed of humility, we will reap the harvest of God's grace. God will answer the door on our behalf. Pride refuses to let God into some areas of the house. But if you will humble yourself like David and sow the seed of humility, He will show grace and bring about restoration. God will start to rebuild your life once again. The choice is yours. You can remain in your pride and be unhappy and unholy, or you can humble yourself and let God begin to rebuild just like he did with Moses, Elijah, and David.

**Augustine was once asked what were
the four cardinal virtues?**
He responded, "Humility, humility, humility, and humility."

IMPERFECT PEOPLE ACCOMPLISH GOD'S PERFECT WILL

One day, I was being interviewed by a media outlet about the 2024 United States Presidential election between President Donald Trump and Vice-President Kamala Harris. The reporter asked me if God could use someone as flawed as Donald Trump to accomplish His perfect will? My response was simple: God only uses flawed people to accomplish His perfect will.

Oftentimes, we forget when hard-working and well-intentioned people like David mess up in a major way and we easily forget that God can still use them. Remember, God used David the adulterer and murderer. He used Moses, too, despite his past. And he can use YOU, no matter what you have done in your past.

God can and God will use YOU too!

THE WAY THINGS OUGHT TO BE

CHAPTER 4

"May the God of hope fill you with all joy and peace as you trust in Him."

— Romans 15:13

Thus far, I hope you have come to the realization that happiness is a necessary ingredient to live out the successful Christian life of holiness. We know that in God's presence there is the fullness of joy and at His right hand there are innumerable pleasures. By positioning ourselves in God's presence, only then will our hearts find true happiness, peace, and harmony. In other words, the way things ought to be. What I just described is the picture of the Hebrew word: **Shalom.**

Shalom is one of the richest words in the Hebrew language. We often simplify its meaning to be merely "peace", but it encompasses much more than just a cease-fire between enemies. Shalom entails flourishing, wholeness, and delight. The best definition I can give for Shalom is quite frankly, things being the way things ought to be. We cannot be truly happy until we can utter the beautiful words with all sincerity, "It is well with my soul."

How do we reach this beautiful state of wholeness, happiness and holiness? I believe there are two pathways that help us arrive at this destination. Both pathways require a heart posture of humility rather than pride. The first pathway towards Shalom is prayer. The second pathway towards Shalom is praise. Both prayer and praise are acts of humility. Both prayer and praise lead us into the very presence of God. Both prayer and praise produce happiness and holiness in our lives.

IF IN PAIN THEN PRAY

One could easily argue that one of the greatest gifts God ever gave humanity is the ability to pray. Think about this for a moment. The God of the Universe allows fallen, finite and fickle creatures like us who are nothing more than a speck in the universe to have an audience with Him. That's mind-blowing. Most people would do almost anything to have an audience with the President of the United States, or the King of England, yet all of us have something far greater. We have an open-door policy with the King of Kings and Lord of Lords. The old hymn sings, "Satan trembles when he sees the weakest saint upon his knees." Why does Satan tremble when we pray? Because there is a real power in prayer.

What is prayer? First, prayer is not an information session to bring God up to date on the affairs of our lives. God already knows. Prayer is not to inform God but to involve God in our lives. That is why prayer is an act of humility. When we come to God in prayer we are showing our total dependence upon Him. Secondly, prayer does not make God do what He does not want to do. Prayer simply moves God to do what He already wanted to do.

In the Book of Acts, there is a repeated theme of an Apostle like Peter or Paul being arrested and imprisoned followed by a prayer and praise session which then produced a miraculous escape through an angel or an earthquake. One of those instances happened early on with Peter and John being arrested and then released. It says in **Acts 4:31**, **"After they prayed, the place where**

112

they were meeting was shaken. And they were all filled with the Holy Spirit and spoke the word of God boldly."

I would like to pray prayers that shake the room. Not the half-hearted, "Lord, bless this food" type of prayer. Instead, I want to pray powerful prayers. This type of prayer is taught prayer. One of the reasons that people struggle to pray is that they have never been taught how to pray. I firmly believe that when we are taught how to pray, we will make prayer as common and natural in our lives as breathing air.

There was a moment in the ministry of Jesus that His disciples asked Him to teach them how to pray. Jesus responded to them that when they pray, they should pray like this:

"Our Father In Heaven, Hallowed Be Your Name. Your Kingdom Come and Your Will Be Done On Earth As It Is In Heaven. Give Us This Day Our Daily Bread and Forgive Us Our Sins As We Forgive Those Who Have Sinned Against Us. Lead Us Not Into Temptation But Deliver Us From The Evil One. For Yours Is The Kingdom, The Power and the Glory Forever Amen."

– Matthew 6:9-13

We refer to this as the Lord's Prayer. A better title would be the Disciple's Prayer, as this is the model and framework that Jesus gave for His disciples to pray. This guide of how to pray begins with God (Father, Name, Kingdom), then moves to us (day, bread, forgiveness), and finishes with exalting God (Kingdom, Power, Glory). God-Us-God is the flow. Prayer is relational conversation with God.

The first few words are so important: Our Father in Heaven. God is Father. He is Father by position. In the Bible within the family structure, the father has two primary responsibilities. Those primary functions of the father are to protect and to provide for his family. I know there are some reading this right now that did not grow up with a good earthly father who took responsibility for his family. But know this about your Heavenly Father, He takes responsibility for His children. This is important to know because we need to know who we are praying to. Not only is God our Father by position, but He is also in Heaven by location. This means He is not limited to, or bound by, the limitations of this earth like our natural fathers are. Our Heavenly Father can split Red Seas, shut the mouths of lions or feed thousands of people with just a few fish and pieces of bread. This is who we are praying to.

"Is anyone among you in trouble? Let them pray. Is anyone happy? Let them sing songs of praise. [14] Is anyone among

you sick? Let them call the elders of the church to pray over them and anoint them with oil in the name of the Lord. [15] And the prayer offered in faith will make the sick person well; the Lord will raise them up. If they have sinned, they will be forgiven. [16] Therefore confess your sins to each other and pray for each other so that you may be healed. The prayer of a righteous person is powerful and effective. [17] Elijah was a human being, even as we are. He prayed earnestly that it would not rain, and it did not rain on the land for three and a half years. [18] Again he prayed, and the heavens gave rain, and the earth produced its crops."

- James 5:13-18

James tells us that if we are in trouble or suffering then we must pray. In other words, if you are in pain then pray. In fact, you could say that pain is an invitation to pray. Sometimes, God will allow pain to enter into our lives to force us into a position of prayer. James then says, if you are happy you should praise (more on praise later this chapter). In other words, if you are in pain, then you should pray. If you are not in pain, then you should praise. In life, we are either in pain or not in pain. Therefore, in life we should either be praying, or we should be praising. That tells me that God wants to hear from us all day long. At the end of this passage on prayer and praise, James draws our attention to the prophet Elijah. **James 5:17-18** says, **"Elijah was a human being, even as we are. He prayed earnestly that it would not rain, and it did not rain on the land for three and a half years. [18] Again he prayed, and the heavens gave rain, and the earth produced its crops."** Elijah was like us; nothing special or unique about him. But when he prayed for no rain, it did not rain. When he prayed for rain, it rained. We saw in the previous chapter the encounter between Elijah and Ahab in the palace that brought about the three and a half years of no rain. But look at the prayer of Elijah that brought rain back to the land of Israel.

"So Ahab went off to eat and drink, but Elijah climbed to the top of Carmel, bent down to the ground and put his face between his knees. [43] "Go and look toward the sea," he told his servant. And he went up and looked. "There is nothing there," he said. Seven times Elijah said, "Go back." [44] The seventh time the servant reported, "A cloud as small as a man's hand is rising from the sea." So Elijah said, "Go and tell Ahab, 'Hitch up your chariot and go down before the rain stops you.'" [45] Meanwhile, the sky grew black with clouds, the wind rose, a heavy rain started falling and Ahab rode off to Jezreel. [46] The power of the Lord came on Elijah and, tucking his cloak into his belt, he ran ahead of Ahab all the way to Jezreel."
- 1 Kings 18:42-46

Did you notice the strange physical position that Elijah took when he prayed? He placed his head between his knees and bent down. Pause in reading this. Go ahead and try that position out! Good luck... Now that you are back, I bet it was awkward and uncomfortable. The reason for that is because the position of Elijah was the position a birthing mother in ancient times would take when it was time to give birth. Why did Elijah take the position of a birthing woman? Because prayer is giving birth to the will of God in heaven here on earth. It is through prayer that we give birth to God's will in our life. Praying is literally pulling down the will of God from heaven to earth. And just like a woman giving birth, when we pray, we have to push and push and push until the process is complete. Elijah prayed seven times. People ask, "How many times should I pray about it?" The answer is to pray until it is complete.

When it comes to the promises of God, we are to remind Him continually of those promises. **Isaiah 62:6-7** says, **"I have posted watchmen on your walls, Jerusalem; they will never be silent day or night. You who call on the Lord, give yourselves no rest,** [7] **and give him no rest till he establishes Jerusalem and makes her the praise of the earth."** Once you get this principle it will change your life. God made a promise that He would establish Jerusalem and make her the praise of all the earth. This was a promise made by God. The prophet Isaiah relayed this promise with a command: call forth this promise continually and give God no rest until He accomplishes what He promised. In other words, pray until it is complete. Does God need to be reminded of His promises? No, not at all. We, however, need to be reminded of His promises constantly. Jesus took this Old Testament principle about prayer and reiterated it through a parable.

"Then Jesus told his disciples a parable to show them that they should always pray and not give up. [2] He said: "In a certain town there was a judge who neither feared God nor cared what people thought. [3] And there was a widow in that town who kept coming to him with the plea, 'Grant me justice against my adversary.' [4] "For some time he refused. But finally he said to himself, 'Even though I don't fear God or care what people think, [5] yet because this widow keeps bothering me, I will see that she gets justice, so that she won't eventually come and attack me!'" [6] And the Lord said, "Listen to what the unjust judge says. [7] And will not God bring about justice for his chosen ones, who cry out to him day and night? Will he keep putting them off? [8] I tell you, he will see that they get justice, and quickly. However, when the Son of Man comes, will he find faith on the earth?"

– Luke 18:1-8

Prayer is to be relentless. We are told to relentlessly remind God of His promises. Remember that God is Father and we are His children. If you have children, then you will understand this easily. I have five amazing kids (Hannah, Ashton, Blitz, Eva & Laken).

There have been times that I have made a promise to them that we would go get ice cream. When I make that promise to them, they believe me. However, my kids will hound me until the promise of ice cream is complete. God says that is exactly how we are to be with Him because He is our Father.

It is through prayer that the dysfunctional things in our life become functional, and those things that are in disharmony find harmony. We experience Shalom through prayer. By continually reminding God of His promises to us, we will see things become the way they ought to be. The result of this will be happiness, peace and contentment. Which should always lead to praise.

IF NOT IN PAIN THEN PRAISE

An interesting truth to ponder upon is that the largest book in the Bible, the Book of Psalms, is all about praise. Why is that? Like prayer, praise is a sacred path into the presence of God. For God inhabits and dwells in the midst of the praises of His people (Psalm 22:3). God takes great pleasure when His people praise Him, you could even say it makes Him happy. But we can learn from our Hebrew forefathers that God is no fan of when His people complain and grumble against Him.

There are a few books in the Bible that hardly anyone reads like Leviticus that have some rich principles that we can learn from (Leviticus is the graveyard of the one-year Bible reading plans). The Book of Numbers is one of those rich, but not read books. This book is often called the book of journeying since it covers the forty-year period of the Hebrew people wandering in the wilderness. Others refer to this book as the book of murmuring because the theme throughout it is the people of God complain over and over again. It is quite amazing that these former slaves of Egypt consistently gripe about their circumstances. Let me paint the picture for you.

Jacob and his twelve sons and their families totaling seventy people moved to Egypt after discovering that their long-lost brother Joseph was the Prime Minister. The offspring of Jacob stayed in Egypt for nearly four hundred years. Unfortunately, over those four centuries they found themselves as slaves in Egypt, yet they multiplied rapidly. By the time of Moses and the Exodus there were roughly over two-million Hebrews in Egypt. The Bible says that God heard the cries of His people and He raised up Moses as their deliverer. Through Moses, God unleashed ten devastating plagues on the richest and most powerful Empire at that time. Things got so bad that the Egyptians begged the Hebrew people to leave and the Hebrew people left Egypt with the gold and silver of the Egyptians (Exodus 12:35-36). In other words, these former slaves left Egypt filthy rich. Not only did they leave Egypt free from the bondages of slavery with great wealth but they were also incredibly healthy. In fact, there was not one sick person among the two-million Hebrews (Psalm

105:37). God was good to the Hebrew people. They were no longer slaves, but they were free, wealthy, and healthy. Most people would praise God for those blessings.

God's goodness continued to be poured out upon the Hebrew people when they left Egypt and headed towards the Promised Land. To journey from Egypt to Canaan by foot, with a very large group of people, would have been about a two-week journey through the desert. An obvious problem about marching two-million people on a two-week journey was feeding them and their livestock. Not many fast-food options in the desert, **but God**. Two words that make all the difference. God sent down miracle food from heaven every single day for six days each week called Manna and the food crisis was solved.

However, weather conditions in the desert were not ideal. In the desert it was scorching hot by day and brutally cold by night. To address these conditions, God did another miracle. He gave the Hebrew people a cloud by day and a pillar of fire by night. The cloud during the day provided shade. The pillar of fire by night provided warmth. What a good God the Hebrew people served and we serve today.

So here is the picture: the Hebrew people were no longer slaves, they were wealthy and healthy, they had miracle food falling from the sky and they had temperature control in the desert. One would assume these blessings from the Most High would produce great shouts of praise. Yet, the Book of Numbers repeatedly points out how the Hebrew people rather than praising God, complained and grumbled against Him and His servant Moses.

"Now the people complained about their hardships in the hearing of the Lord, and when he heard them his anger was aroused. Then fire from the Lord burned among them and consumed some of the outskirts of the camp. ² When the people cried out to Moses, he prayed to the Lord and the fire died down."

- Numbers 11:1-2

The Lord heard not praise but complaints. God was not pleased with what He heard, yet Moses prayed for the people, and the wrath of God relented. Unfortunately, this heart posture of complaining from the Hebrew people persisted.

"The Lord said to Moses and Aaron: ²⁷ "How long will this wicked community grumble against me? I have heard the complaints of these grumbling Israelites. ²⁸ So tell them, 'As surely as I live, declares the Lord, I will do to you the very thing I heard you say: ²⁹ In this wilderness your bodies will fall—every one of you twenty years old or more who was

counted in the census and who has grumbled against me.
30 Not one of you will enter the land I swore with uplifted
hand to make your home, except Caleb son of Jephunneh and
Joshua son of Nun."

- Numbers 14:26-30

How sad it is to read about how the first generation of
Hebrews free from slavery in Egypt were not allowed to enter the
Promised Land because of their complaining. May that serve as
a lesson to us. **Praise attracts the manifest presence of God but
complaining repels Him.** After the first generation died in the
wilderness, Moses who was now one-hundred and twenty years
old gave a farewell speech to the second generation of Hebrews
who would enter the Promised Land.

The farewell speech of Moses is recorded for us as the Book
of Deuteronomy. Which is the retelling of the Law to the next
generation. Moses wanted to make sure that the new generation
did not repeat the same mistakes as their parents.

"Be careful to follow every command I am giving you today,
so that you may live and increase and may enter and possess
the land the Lord promised on oath to your ancestors. [2]
Remember how the Lord your God led you all the way in
the wilderness these forty years, to humble and test you in
order to know what was in your heart, whether or not you

would keep his commands. [3] He humbled you, causing you to hunger and then feeding you with manna, which neither you nor your ancestors had known, to teach you that man does not live on bread alone but on every word that comes from the mouth of the Lord. [4] Your clothes did not wear out and your feet did not swell during these forty years. [5] Know then in your heart that as a man disciplines his son, so the Lord your God disciplines you. [6] Observe the commands of the Lord your God, walking in obedience to him and revering him. [7] For the Lord your God is bringing you into a good land—a land with brooks, streams, and deep springs gushing out into the valleys and hills; [8] a land with wheat and barley, vines and fig trees, pomegranates, olive oil and honey; [9] a land where bread will not be scarce and you will lack nothing; a land where the rocks are iron and you can dig copper out of the hills. [10] When you have eaten and are satisfied, praise the Lord your God for the good land he has given you. [11] Be careful that you do not forget the Lord your God, failing to observe his commands, his laws and his decrees that I am giving you this day. [12] Otherwise, when you eat and are satisfied, when you build fine houses and settle down, [13] and when your herds and flocks grow large and your silver and gold increase and all you have is multiplied, [14] then your heart will become proud and you will forget the Lord your God, who brought you out of Egypt, out of the land of slavery. [15] He led you through the vast and dreadful wilderness, that thirsty and waterless land, with its venomous snakes and scorpions. He brought you water out of hard rock. [16] He gave you manna to eat in the wilderness, something your ancestors had never known, to humble and test you so that in the end it might go well with you. [17] You may say to yourself, "My power and the strength of my hands have produced this wealth for me." [18] But remember the Lord your God, for it is he who gives you the ability to produce wealth, and so confirms his covenant, which he swore to your ancestors, as it is today."

- Deuteronomy 8:1-18

Read Deuteronomy 8:10 one more time: "**When you have eaten and are satisfied, praise the Lord your God for the good land he has given you.**" Moses went on to say that if you do not praise God for His goodness, the result will be that your heart will grow proud. When we taste the goodness of the Lord, it is imperative that we respond with praise. Otherwise, we will fool ourselves into believing that we are the cause of the good things in our lives.

Recall the time when ten lepers came to Jesus and asked to be healed. Jesus healed all ten but only one came back to give Jesus thanks. What we find out is all ten were healed of leprosy but only one was made whole. Only one experienced Shalom. People believe that once they become whole then they will be grateful, but it is being grateful that makes us whole. Instead of complaining about life, choose to give praise and thanksgiving to God for the gift of life. The quotable Mark Twain once said,

126

"Don't complain to people about your problems. 80% of people don't care, and the other 20% believe you got what you deserve."

Maybe your praise to God is past due. Quick example of what I mean by that. I have the privilege to pastor a great church in Oklahoma and every month our church shows our appreciation to the electric company for being so good by providing us with power. However, one month we forgot to show our appreciation (we did not pay our bill) to the electric company and we got a letter in the mail with a past due notice. There could be a very high probability that God's power in your life seems to be turned off because your praise is way past due. Therefore, let everything that has breath Praise the Lord (Psalm 150:6).

"Praise the Lord from the heavens; praise him in the heights above. ² Praise him, all his angels; praise him, all his heavenly hosts. ³ Praise him, sun and moon; praise him, all you shining stars. ⁴ Praise him, you highest heavens and you waters above the skies"

- Psalm 148:1-4

THE ULTIMATE CHASE

CONCLUSION

"The joy of the Lord is your strength"
– Nehemiah 8:10

We have reached the end of this journey together in the pursuit of finding happiness so that we can live out holiness before the Lord. I must admit that the creation of this book has probably blessed me more than anyone who will ever read it. There is an old saying that if you want to learn a subject then teach it. I will add to it that if you really want to learn about a subject then write a book about it.

I love stories because as a preacher of the Gospel, I know how powerful stories are. Therefore, let me leave you with one more. Years ago, there was a man who loved to collect rare and valuable pieces of art. He had one son who joined the military to serve his country. One day, a battle broke out involving his platoon and a fellow soldier was struck down on the battlefield. The son of that wealthy man charged into the frenzy to rescue his friend. In the process of bringing his friend back to safety, the wealthy man's son was hit and died on the battlefield as a hero. The message was sent to the father that his son died a hero's death serving his country, but as you can imagine this just devastated the man.

However, several months later there was a knock at the door of the father's house and when he opened the door, there stood a soldier in uniform. The soldier said, "Sir, you do not know me, but your son saved my life by giving his and he would always tell us how much you loved to collect art. I painted a portrait of your son on the battlefield as a hero and wanted to give it to you." This brought the man to tears as he embraced the soldier and gladly received the painting. That painting actually became the prized piece of art in his very extensive collection.

The day came when the wealthy man passed away, and his entire art collection went up for auction. On the night of the auction, the room was packed with potential and eager collectors. The auctioneer stepped up to the podium with all the rare and valuable pieces of art on stage behind him and announced,

"Ladies and gentleman, this man stipulated in his will that we start this auction with his favorite piece of art. It is a painting done by a soldier of his son as a hero on the battlefield." As he announced the first piece of art to be auctioned off there was no real buzz in the room. The auctioneer asked for $500 and nobody bid. He then dropped it down to $100 and somebody raised their hand and after going once, twice, and three times that piece of art was sold for $100.

At the conclusion of that piece being sold the auctioneer then announced, "Ladies and gentleman, that concludes tonight's auction." Suddenly, there were gasps and shouts of questions from the crowd, "What about all the other pieces of rare and valuable art? That is why we are here!" The auctioneer quieted the crowd and said, "The man stipulated in his will that whoever got the painting of his son would also get everything else with it."

Everyone in life wants the rare and valuable pieces of art on the stage such as happiness, love, peace, contentment, fulfillment, and so forth. But all of those things are attached to the Son. Whoever gets the Son will also get everything else with Him. Do you desire peace? Seek the Son who is the Prince of Peace. Desire love? Seek Jesus who is Love. Desire joy? Seek God whose very presence is the fullness of joy. It might be the cliché Sunday

School answer, but Jesus is the answer to all of our wants, needs, and desires. It is my prayer that this simple and short book has hopefully sparked a desire in your heart to pursue Jesus.

ULTIMATE PRACTICAL GUIDE TO HAPPINESS

PT. 1

HOW TO HEAR GOD'S VOICE

I want to share briefly about discovering how to hear from God. God has not lost his voice. He still speaks today. Jesus said in **John 10:27**, that His sheep know His voice. Hearing the voice of God, though, is something that takes time to develop. Having been in ministry and teaching at different Bible colleges, I have been asked a lot of questions over the years. One of the top questions I get asked most often is, "How do I hear the voice of God?" That is a question that so many people struggle with.

To hear from God, we must first slow down and pause to listen. Talking to God is like using a walkie-talkie. Remember using walkie-talkies as a kid? For the walkie-talkie to work each person has to be on the right channel. So how do we hear from God on our spiritual walkie-talkies? We must listen and be on the right channel. Some of the channels that God uses to speak is His Word, He uses visions and dreams, and then His audible voice. If you listen on the right channel, He will speak to you. I want to encourage you to listen for the voice of God in your life. **Proverbs 8:34** says, **"Blessed are those who listen to me, watching daily at my doors, waiting at my doorway."**

CHANNEL #1 – THE BIBLE

It is my opinion that God speaks mostly to us through His written Word. Yes, God speaks with His still small voice, He also uses dreams and visions. But God uses His Word to communicate to us on a regular basis. In fact, we can hear from God anytime we want. We just have to open up the Bible and begin to read. The Bible is full of sixty-six different love letters (books) written from God addressed to us. Research shows that nearly nine out of ten households have a Bible. That is a pretty impressive number but sadly only twenty-five percent of Bible owners read their Bible on a regular basis. This has resulted in God's people not knowing God's Word. A funny, but sad, illustration is when a new pastor arrived at a local church to serve and was asked to teach the junior high boys' Sunday school class in the absence of the regular teacher. He decided to see what they knew, so he asked who knocked down the walls of Jericho. All the boys adamantly said, "Pastor, we swear we didn't do it." Unfortunately, too many adult Christians have only a vague familiarity with the Bible.

It is important that we get in the Word of God on a regular basis. God wants so badly to communicate with us. But in communication there are four facets. There is the communicator, there is the message, there is the channel, and there is the recipient. All four are necessary for communication to take place. God wants to communicate with us and He has a message for us and the Bible is the primary, although not only channel that He uses to speak to us through.

Paul says in **Romans 10:17** that, "**Consequently, faith comes from hearing the message, and the message is heard through the word about Christ.**" Other translations will say that faith comes by hearing and hearing the Word of God. Both are saying the exact same thing. When we hear the message of Christ, which is the Gospel, our faith is being built. When we are faithful in hearing God's Word our faith rises and rises. We do not want our faith to be stagnant and dead but alive and growing. Our faith grows by hearing the Word of God, but sometimes we get lax and caught up in the busyness of life and are not intentional and focused on being in the Word. It happens to all of us in life. Let me challenge you to get in the Book, and let the Book get in you. The brilliant, C.S. Lewis said, "The enemy will put a good book in front of you to distract you from the Great Book." There is nothing wrong with reading books about the Bible, but if those are the only books we are reading then we are missing out. I pray that reading this book will in fact motivate you to read the Bible more than what you did before reading this book.

I ran into this problem when I was a student at Oral Roberts University. I was a theology major reading a lot of books about the Bible yet ironically, I forgot to read the actual Bible. I remember a professor once saying, "What does it profit you to get A's in all your courses, but to flunk life in the process." That spoke to me, and I knew I needed to get back into the habit of reading the Word.

The Word of God is a lamp unto our feet and light unto our path. It is sweeter than honey and it is more desirable than gold. It is by the power of God's Word that sinners become saints and broken people become whole people. God's Word is the key that unlocks hardened hearts. The Word of God is a bed for us to rest upon. Although the Word has faced banishment and persecution it remains. It is indestructible and forever settled in heaven. For the grass may fade and the flower may wither, but the Word of our God will stand forever. Charles Spurgeon who was one of the greatest theologians during the 1800's has one of the most famous quotes about the Bible of all time. He said, "If your Bible is falling apart, then your life probably is not. But if your Bible is not falling apart then your life probably is." So, I have something for you to think about: What does your Bible look like?

We want to build our lives on God's Word. It is important for us to have the Bible as our foundation in life because our foundations determine how high we can build. If you want to build a skyscraper high in the sky you must first dig deep down in the ground and make sure you have a solid foundation to build upon. Your foundation is like the roots of a plant. If you want your life to rise high in the sky and you want to soar with eagles, then you have to make sure you have a solid root system and a solid foundation. The fruit that you bear in your life is a result of your foundation; it is a result of your root system. Deep roots produce much fruit. But because roots are out of sight they are often out of mind. No one drives by a big, beautiful house and focuses on

140

the foundation, but the foundation is vital. Your foundation is who you are underneath. It is what you believe at your core. God wants to make sure that you have a solid foundation that is built on His Word; that you have a healthy root system. Roots serve as an anchor for a tree or plant. When winds, rains, and floods come it is the root system that keeps a tree in place so that it is not washed or blown away. If a tree is not securely planted in the ground when a storm comes it will be uprooted and it will die. In life you will experience storms, but if you are planted and your roots are down deep you will withstand the storms of life. When the winds blow and the floods rise you will not be moved. We want to be planted and rooted in God's Word.

Isaiah 55:10-11 says, "As the rain and the snow come down from heaven, and do not return to it without watering the earth and making it bud and flourish, so that it yields seed for the Sower and bread for the eater, so is my word that goes out from my mouth: It will not return to me empty, but will accomplish what I desire and achieve the purpose for which I sent it."

Just as the rain comes down and does what it is supposed to do on the earth. God says His Word is like the rain. When He sends His Word it accomplishes what it is supposed to accomplish. If you read the Bible, it will change you. "Yeah, but Jackson, I have read the Bible before and nothing has ever happened." An evangelist named Gipsy Smith was once talking with a person who told him the same thing that he had read through the Bible several times, and nothing ever happened to him. Gipsy Smith told the man "Let the Bible go through you once instead of you going through it and see what happens. Then you will tell a different story!" Let's not just go through the Word, but let the Word go through us. If you are new to the Bible, I suggest that you start reading with the Gospel of John and then the Book of Genesis. It is also VITAL that you get connected to a solid Bible based church so that you can grow and flourish.

CHANNEL #2 – VISIONS, DREAMS & IMAGES

Another channel that God will speak to us through is visions, dreams, and images. **Joel 2:28** says, **"I will pour out my Spirit on all people. Your sons and daughters will prophesy, your old men will dream dreams, your young men will see visions.** [29] **Even on my servants, both men and women, I will pour out my Spirit in those days."** God speaks through the channel of visions and dreams. I can recall when I was a freshman at Oral Roberts University, I was driving to class one morning, and I had a vision while driving. I began at ORU as a business major because I wanted to own my own business. Well, I felt called into ministry however business is what I had chosen. While driving to class I had this incredible vision of me being in ministry and I saw things into the future that were beyond me with vivid details. Not sure what to make of it, I went to class with that vision not knowing whether or not it was from God or something I was dreaming up myself. Later that evening I went to church and responded to the altar call. An older gentleman came up to pray for me and prophesied to me the exact vision I had earlier that morning (God also uses His people to speak to us). This was enough to convince me and so I went in soon after and made the switch from a business major to a theology major and answered the call into ministry. God speaks to His people through visions, dreams, images, and mental pictures. This happened throughout the Bible and it still happens today. Ask God to speak to you through this channel.

CHANNEL #3 – GOD'S AUDIBLE VOICE

A third way that God speaks to His people is through His own Voice. Now this is rarer and it may not happen every single day of your life but God does have a distinct voice. Sometimes it is a still small voice that speaks quietly to our hearts while other times it may be an incredibly loud voice that is like thunder during the Oklahoma spring season. God has a voice and He has not lost it. If we listen closely, His voice will speak to us. **Proverbs 8:34** says, **"Blessed are those who listen to me, watching daily at my doors, waiting at my doorway."**

HOW TO TEST IF IT IS FROM GOD

Now you might be wondering, "How can I be sure that I am hearing from God?" There are a few principles we can utilize to test whether or not it is God, the Devil, or our own imagination.

TEST #1 - GOD'S VOICE WILL NEVER CONTRADICT HIS WORD

The first test to always apply is whether or not what you are hearing aligns with or against the Bible. In **Psalm 89:34** God says, **"I will not violate my covenant or alter what my lips have uttered."** God's voice will never contradict His Word. Therefore, if you are hearing something on the inside of you telling you to do something that goes against God's Word then you can safely know that is not God. However, in order to know if what you are hearing contradicts the Word, you have to know the Word. That is why I will emphasize again being grounded in the Bible and a good Bible centered church.

TEST #2 – GOD'S VOICE WILL NEVER TEMPT YOU TO SIN

Test number 2, God's voice will never tempt you to sin. If you sense something telling you to go steal the Blackstone Grill from your neighbor's backyard, that isn't God, that is either the enemy or your own greed and covetousness speaking. **James 1:13** says, **"When tempted, no one should say, "God is tempting me." For God cannot be tempted by evil, nor does he tempt anyone."** God's voice will never tempt you to sin.

TEST #3 – GOD'S VOICE WILL BE CONFIRMED BY HIS PEOPLE

Lastly, God's Voice will be confirmed by God's people. When I believe I am hearing from God, I will always share it with a few close and trusted believers. I do not recommend sharing with just anybody and everybody but a few people that you know also hear from God. **Proverbs 11:14** says, **"For lack of guidance a nation falls, but victory is won through many advisers."** It is so important to have a multitude of counselors. This is why we have to also develop solid relationships (see Ultimate Practical Guide To Happiness PT. II).

An example of this came in my life when I was a new Pastor struggling with a barely surviving church. Shortly after, I was offered a position to lead a Bible College at a very large church. It was very appealing to me because at the time there seemed to be no hope for Sheridan.Church. Both Kendra and I agreed that we should take the new role and resign as the Lead Pastors of Sheridan.Church. But one evening I went to a church service to hear Pastor Jentzen Franklin preach. His sermon came from his latest book at the time entitled "*Acres of Diamonds.*" I would highly recommend that you read this book.

In summary, there was a man who had a farm but could not get anything to grow because of all the rocks. He got wind that there was gold to be found in a river over in India. He left his farm and went to India to discover there was not any gold at all. Another man purchased that farm and ran into the same problem, too many rocks. The new farmer found one of the rocks that was quite large and placed it on the mantle of his fireplace. One day a visitor came by and saw the rock and said, "Sir, do you know what that is?" The new farmer said, "I have no idea but those rocks are everywhere." The man responded, "That is a diamond in the rough." Long story short, that farmland was full of acres of diamonds. One man left too soon and missed out.

While Jentzen was preaching, I thought I heard God's voice say that Sheridan was full of acres of diamonds and that I needed to stay. Suddenly, I received a text from a friend who was at the same service and was aware that I was planning on leaving Sheridan. He text me the following:

SN

Steve >

Acres of Diamonds.
Its in your House.

Sounds like prophetic words
for Sheridan

That night, God spoke to me. Kendra and I decided to stay at Sheridan.Church and I am so glad that we did. The only reason I am still the Pastor of Sheridan is because God spoke directly to me. We all have to make decisions in life. We all need to hear God's voice.

CONCLUSION

God wants to speak to you. He will speak to you through the Bible, through dreams, visions, as well as His voice. We can know if it is from God if it does not contradict His written Word, if it does not tempt us to sin, and if it is confirmed by His people. But in order to hear the voice of God we must pray.

Here is an acronym for you about prayer. **ACTS**:

A is for adoration. When you start your prayers do not start with my name is Jimmie so give me, give me, give me. No, adore God and proclaim who He is and how great He is.

C is for confession. We must confess our sins before God and He is faithful and just to forgive them.

T is for thanksgiving. We enter into His courts with thanksgiving.

S is for supplication. We make our requests known to God.

ACTS:

Adoration, Confession, Thanksgiving, & Supplication.

ULTIMATE PRACTICAL GUIDE TO HAPPINESS

PT. 3

HOW TO FORGIVE

My favorite book in the Bible is Philemon. It is a letter written by Paul to Philemon who was his friend. This obscure New Testament letter is about half a page right before the book of Hebrews. Philemon is my favorite book of the Bible because I love the story within it and I believe that the entire Gospel message is wrapped up in that half of a page.

Context: Philemon had a church that met in his house during the first century in the Roman Empire. During the first century churches did not meet in nice auditoriums, instead they met at believer's houses, and also in the catacombs to be under the radar from the Roman authorities. Philemon had a house church, and

Philemon was a man of his culture and had several slaves. Now slavery in the Roman Empire was vastly different than slavery in the Americas during the 18th and 19th centuries. In the Roman Empire, one out of every three persons was a slave. Now the institution of slavery is evil, but the form of slavery in the Roman Empire allowed for people to sell themselves into slavery for a period to pay off debt or whatever it may be.

Philemon had a slave named Onesimus. We are not sure what Onesimus did, but he did something wrong and ran away. Most believe he stole from Philemon. Onesimus ran away and ended up in the same prison where Paul the Apostle was in chains. How this relationship between Paul and Onesimus developed, we are not sure, but Paul being the evangelist that he was, witnessed to Onesimus in that Roman prison and Onesimus gave his life to Christ. At some point, in prison together, Paul and Onesimus realized they both knew Philemon. In fact, Philemon got saved under Paul's ministry and was a dear friend of his.

Paul recognized that although he was locked up in physical chains that Onesimus was locked up in spiritual chains because of the broken relationship between him and Philemon. Paul told Onesimus that he must go back and reconcile with Philemon. I imagine that Onesimus probably fought it. But Paul was persistent and insisted that Onesimus make things right with Philemon. In order to help reconcile Philemon and Onesimus, Paul wrote a letter and we have it in our New Testament. It is the Book of Philemon.

"Paul, a prisoner of Christ Jesus, and Timothy our brother, To Philemon our dear friend and fellow worker— [2] also to Apphia our sister and Archippus our fellow soldier—and to the church that meets in your home: [3] Grace and peace to you from God our Father and the Lord Jesus Christ. [4] I always thank my God as I remember you in my prayers, [5] because I hear about your love for all his holy people and your faith in the Lord Jesus. [6] I pray that your partnership with us in the faith may be effective in deepening your understanding of every good thing we share for the sake of Christ. [7] Your love has given me great joy and encouragement, because you, brother, have refreshed the hearts of the Lord's people. [8] Therefore, although in Christ I could be bold and order you to do what you ought to do, [9] yet I prefer to appeal to you on the basis of love. It is as none other than Paul—an old man and now also a prisoner of Christ Jesus— [10] that I appeal to you for my son Onesimus, who became my son while I was in chains. [11] Formerly he was useless to you, but now he has become useful both to you and to me. [12] I am sending him— who is my very heart—back to you. [13] I would have liked to keep him with me so that he could take your place in helping me while I am in chains for the gospel. [14] But I did not want to do anything without your consent, so that any favor you do would not seem forced but would be voluntary. [15] Perhaps the reason he was separated from you for a little while was that you might have him back forever— [16] no longer as a slave, but better than a slave, as a dear brother. He is very dear to me but even dearer to you, both as a fellow man and as a brother in the Lord. [17] So if you consider me a partner, welcome him as you would welcome me. [18] If he has done you any wrong or owes you anything, charge it to me. [19] I, Paul, am writing this with my own hand. I will pay it back—not to mention that you owe me your very self. [20] I do wish, brother, that I may have some benefit from you in the Lord; refresh my heart in Christ. [21] Confident of your obedience, I write to you, knowing that you will do even more than I ask. [22] And one thing more: Prepare a guest room for me, because I hope to be restored to you in answer to your prayers."

- Philemon 1-22

Paul recognized that both Onesimus and Philemon were broken relationally and in chains spiritually; they were locked up emotionally, relationally, and spiritually. Paul wanted to see them become whole. Paul knew the importance of reconciliation and being in the ministry of reconciliation. Although you are probably not a runaway slave, maybe you are locked up in spiritual chains due to broken relationships in your life. Relationships are tough because fallen people have a tendency to do fallen things to other fallen people. When fallen people do fallen things to other fallen people things can get messy. Relationships take work. Relationships require forgiveness.

FORGIVENESS

Here is the thing, we who have received Christ Jesus as Lord have been forgiven. Think about how often God forgives us? For me it is every day multiple times per day. We all are constantly needing God's forgiveness and thankfully when we confess our sins He forgives us. But you should remember this: **forgiven people are forgiving people**. You might be thinking, "Why should I forgive them though?" That's easy. Because God said so. You don't need any other reason. God said so. Jesus says in **Mark 11:25**, "**And when you stand praying, if you hold anything against anyone, forgive them, so that your Father in heaven may forgive you your sins.**" Did you know unforgiveness brings your prayer life to a screeching stop. Trust me when I say that we need to forgive.

Here is one reason why God wants us to forgive: unforgiveness and bitterness destroy us from the inside out and make us miserable. Unforgiveness and bitterness are two of the heaviest chains we will ever wear in life. They will weigh us down. Bitterness is a true poison that we drink too often. Someone who gets bitter will never get better. In order to get better you have to make sure, you do not get bitter but walk in forgiveness. Unforgiveness and bitterness are like driving a car and only looking in your rear-view mirror. If you are driving a car and you only see what is behind you, then you will have a crash because you are not looking ahead of you. You can either rehearse all the bad things that have happened to you or you can release them. Forgiveness is all about releasing. Forgiveness is releasing the right to get even. When you forgive you set a prisoner free. That prisoner is you.

Let me give you a picture of forgiveness. Picture the Liberty Bell. Imagine someone ringing that bell back and forth. It is ringing louder and louder as it goes faster and faster and suddenly the rope is let go. Although the rope has been let go of, the bell is still ringing but gradually it will slow and the noise will become a little softer until it comes to an end. Forgiveness is something like that. Unforgiveness is taking that rope and swinging back and forth as fast as you can while it continues ringing on the inside of you. Forgiveness is letting go of that rope by faith. But notice that the bell does not just stop immediately. Those feelings will not just instantly go away. But over time it will slow down and the ringing on the inside will quiet down. Forgiveness is like that. It is an act of faith and it is a necessary act if we are to be whole. What you hold onto will always hold you back.

FORGIVENESS IS NOT ABOUT KEEPING SCORE

In **Matthew 18:21-22** it says, **"Then Peter came to Jesus and asked, "Lord, how many times shall I forgive my brother or sister who sins against me? Up to seven times?"** [22] **Jesus answered, "I tell you, not seven times, but seventy-seven times."** When I read this question that Peter asked, it seems as if Peter actually had somebody in mind that he may have forgiven six times previously, and was looking for Jesus to give him permission to write this person off. I have noticed that as Christians we have learned all too well of how to keep count of the number of times someone has hurt us. In fact, we can recall the date, time, and place of where it happened. But the people who tend to hurt us the most are those who we love the most, have helped the most, and feel the closest too. When Peter asks that question, I am sure he thought he was being generous with forgiving seven times but Jesus blows his mind. Jesus says not just seven times but seven times seventy times. In other words, you can never stop forgiving people just as God never stops forgiving you.

As the saying goes, forgiveness is not about keeping score it is about losing count. Right after Jesus was asked this question, he went on to tell what I believe is the most powerful parable in all the Gospels. It is a parable that pierces the heart. Jesus tells his disciples a story about a man who owed the king around ten million dollars. Because the man could not repay the king, the king ordered that he, his wife, and children be sold into slavery to pay for the debt. The man got down on his knees and begged for mercy, "Please your majesty not my kids, or my wife. Please grant us mercy. Be patient with me and I will pay you back." The king felt sorry for the man and showed him mercy and actually cancelled the debt and let him and his family go free.

The man was so happy and thankful. He kissed the king's feet and left with joy. But as soon as he left the king's presence, he ran into a servant of his who owed him three hundred dollars. He grabbed that man by the throat and demanded his three hundred dollars be paid right away without even talking to him. The servant pleaded, "Please be patient with me and show me mercy. I will repay you." That man refused and had his servant tossed in prison. When the king found out what had happened, he called in that man and said, "You wicked servant, I canceled all that debt of yours because you begged me to. You should have had mercy on your fellow servant just as I had on you." And the king had that man thrown in prison. Jesus says at the end of this parable in **Matthew 18:35**, "**This is how my heavenly Father will treat each of you unless you forgive your brother or sister from your heart.**"

Unforgiveness is dangerous. God wants us to walk in forgiveness because unforgiveness and bitterness will destroy us. Let me give you an example of what unforgiveness looks like; think of a treadmill. On a treadmill you are wearing yourself out yet moving absolutely nowhere. You are stuck in the same spot you were except you are pouring down in sweat and are drained physically. You think that you are moving forward when in reality you have gone nowhere. That is what unforgiveness is like. You wear yourself out running in the same place for years. It is a very heavy chain. Forgiveness is an act of faith and it is a necessary act. A lot of times I get asked, "How do I actually forgive someone?" That's a really good question. I want to give you three points on forgiveness. We will call them the 3 C's to Forgiving. They are small things that make a major difference.

#1 - CATCH YOUR THOUGHTS

Number one is to *catch your thoughts*. Did you know that you are in control of what you think? You really are. Watch this: I want you to picture the beach in Florida. Right now, you are seeing the water and the warm sand with the sun shining down. Now I want you to picture an elephant. Now I want you to picture that elephant as a pink elephant. Now I want you to picture the beach again. Get this: in less than a fraction of a second you went from thinking about a pink elephant to a beach in Florida (this example comes from Timothy Keller's book *Attitude Is Everything*). The human mind is an absolutely incredible thing. No computer can do what you just did as quickly as you just did. The vivid imagery you just had is amazing. And all those images were choices you made. You chose to think about and picture the beach. You chose to think about and picture a pink elephant. You have the power to change your thoughts. Therefore, when negative thoughts arise about that person that hurt you, make the decision to catch your thoughts. Paul says in **2nd Corinthians 10:4-5**, **"The weapons we fight with are not the weapons of the world. On the contrary, they have divine power to demolish strongholds. ⁵ We demolish arguments and every pretension that sets itself up against the knowledge of God, and we take captive every thought to make it obedient to Christ."** How do we capture every thought? That leads to the second C.

#2 - CHANGE YOUR WORDS

Number two is you have to change your words. In order to capture your thoughts, you will have to change your words. What you say and hear you will eventually come to believe. Your words are powerful. They can be used to build yourself and people up, or they can be used to tear yourself and people down. Words can bring life and encouragement or they can bring death and destruction. Words are powerful! **Proverbs 18:20-21** says this, **"From the fruit of their mouth a person's stomach is filled; with the harvest of their lips they are satisfied. Death and life are in the power of the tongue, and those who love it will eat its fruits."** You are going to eat what you say. Therefore, do not digest unhealthy words. When you have the opportunity to speak bad about that person who has hurt you, make the decision to restrain yourself. Forgiveness does not speak ill of those who have hurt us because our words matter. **Proverbs 6:2** says, **"You have been trapped by what you have said; ensnared by the words of your mouth**." Sometimes we get hung by our tongue or tripped by our lip. Forgiveness catches our thoughts, changes our words, and lastly commits our actions.

#3 COMMIT YOUR ACTIONS

When we choose to catch our thoughts and change our words we also need to commit our actions. Paul says in **Ephesians 4:31-32, "Get rid of all bitterness, rage and anger, brawling and slander, along with every form of malice. [32] Be kind and**

compassionate to one another, forgiving each other, just as in Christ God forgave you." There is a possibility that you are holding onto past hurts from family members or friends who did you wrong. They were wrong but you still have to forgive. You have been forgiven a ten-million-dollar debt. The least you can do is forgive your father, mother, brother, or sister a three-hundred-dollar debt. God is pleading with you to forgive them because He wants you whole.

When King Saul had his kingship torn away from him and given to David by God, Saul on numerous occasions tried to have David killed. David spent many years on the run because of Saul and you would think that is enough to harbor some bitterness considering Saul tried having him killed for years. When Saul died and David assumed the throne, he wanted to know if there were relatives of Saul still alive in the land. Now this was a usual practice when one king took over from another. The new king would hunt down the family members of the dethroned king and have them executed so there could be no claim to the throne. So, you would think David would follow that procedure especially since Saul chased him for years.

But look at <u>2nd Samuel 9:1</u>, **"David asked, "Is there still anyone left of the house of Saul to whom I may show kindness** for Jonathan's sake?" Jonathan was the son of Saul and was very close to David. Instead of hunting down Saul's family to kill them, David hunted them down to bless them because of Saul's son. Look at **2nd Samuel 9:7**, David found a grandson of Saul and this is what he said, "**David said to him, "Do not be afraid, for I will show you kindness for the sake of your father Jonathan; I will restore to you all the land of your grandfather Saul, and you yourself shall eat at my table always.**" Is that not the perfect picture of grace and forgiveness? Kind of like how we get to sit at the Table of the Father because of the act of forgiveness by the shedding of blood of the Son. David practically lived out walking in forgiveness.

There was a time in my life that I had to implement these 3 C's. Ministry is difficult. People you never expect to betray you actually do. It is wild. Once, I was told by a great Pastor that "If you won't get bitter then you will make it in the ministry."

There came a time when I found myself bitter. A married couple in our church had worked their way up through the church into leadership. Suddenly, they went from singing my praises to accusing me of having demons... yes demons. They tried to lead a church split and start their own church out of Sheridan. It hurt and I was upset. I would consistently catch my thoughts and change my words regarding them but I was still bitter. One Saturday night, as I was preparing to preach on forgiveness and going over my notes about the 3 C's, I sensed the Lord leading me to bless the ministry of the couple that tried to cause a church split. It was a tough pill to swallow, but I knew it was necessary, not for them, but for me.

I called my best friend and Associate Pastor, John Killian, and said I needed a huge favor. I asked him to call the couple and bless them that night. This is why having godly friends is so important. John did not try talking me out of it but agreed it was a necessary move and he did it. That Sunday morning, when I preached about forgiveness there was a fresh authenticity coming from it and it was one of the most powerful altar calls I have ever experienced. Forgiveness blesses the forgiver in ways that I do not think we truly understand.

CONCLUSION

I want to finish this section by reading what Jesus says in **Matthew 6:14-15**, **"For if you forgive other people when they sin against you, your heavenly Father will also forgive you.** [15] **But if you do not forgive others their sins, your Father will not forgive your sins."** I have always been taught that there is only one unforgivable sin. I earned a Bachelors and a Masters degree in Theology and that entire time I just thought there was one unforgivable sin, but I think that there are actually two unforgivable sins. It is unforgivable to be unforgivable. If you choose not to forgive others, then God says He will not forgive you. You receive grace upon giving grace. The amount of grace you give is the amount of grace you will receive.

I do not know about you, but I am not going to choose to go to hell because somebody hurt me. I am going to choose to forgive just as God forgave me. This is serious stuff. We try to cover all this stuff up in our lives. Now this does not mean that you have to be best friends with the person who did you wrong. No need to stick your hand either in the oven or on the stove twice if you already know it will burn you. But when you have the opportunity to hurt that person and you choose not to, that means you have forgiven them.

Unfortunately, sometimes relationships break down like Philemon and Onesimus. It is important we do what we can to bring about reconciliation so that we are not locked up spiritually. If you will apply those three principles, I just gave you, God will work the miracle. Maybe you know in your heart that you have a broken relationship with a family member or a friend and it is time to make it right. It is time to be freed of those chains.

In order for you to be whole you have to begin with your relationship with God. Just as the relationship between Philemon and Onesimus was broken, so was the relationship between God and humanity. I believe that the story contained within Philemon is a perfect picture of the Gospel. Here you have Philemon the master and Onesimus the servant. Onesimus the servant ran away and separated himself from his master. Then comes a mediator of reconciliation, the Apostle Paul, who told Philemon anything that Onesimus owes you, charge it to my account so that his debt can be paid and you two can be reconciled. Kind of like how humanity separated itself from God the master, but Jesus Christ the second member of the Holy Trinity says to the Father, anything they have done charge it to my account and I will repay their debt. There is good news, Jesus paid the debt! You no longer have to be separated from your heavenly Father. And those of us who have been reconciled have the privilege like Paul to be ministers of reconciliation. Be forgiven and choose to forgive.

ULTIMATE PRACTICAL GUIDE TO HAPPINESS

PT. 2

HOW TO BUILD FULFILLING RELATIONSHIPS

It has been correctly said that if you get your relationships right you will get life right; you will experience happiness, peace, and fulfillment. But if you get your friends wrong you will get your life wrong; you will experience pain, heartache, and even destruction. There is a popular saying today that is so true. The saying is this: "Show me your friends and I will show you your future." Who you choose to do life with really does matter. The Bible actually taught this concept thousands of years ago. Solomon said in **Proverbs 13:20**, "**Walk with the wise and become wise, for a companion of fools suffers harm.**" You become who you hang around. Denzel Washington once said that "if you hang around five intelligent people then you will be the sixth. If you hang around five millionaires, then you will be the sixth. But if you hang around five idiots then you will be the sixth." I say in response to that, AMEN!

4 TYPES OF RELATIONSHIPS

Relationships are interesting because some give life to us, while others take life out from us. There are four types of relationships that we will experience in life. First, there are **adders**. These people add to our life and bring life to us. They are typically our friends. Secondly, there are **subtractors**. These people constantly drain life from us. Then there are **dividers**. These people are big trouble. They bring division and heartache everywhere they go. Did you know, there are times in life that we experience unnecessary pain and suffering because of who we have allowed in our life?

Recall the short story of Jonah. He was told by God to go and preach to the people in Nineveh so they would repent of their sins and God would forgive them. But Jonah hated the people of Nineveh because of what they did to Israel, and he wanted God to punish them. Instead of going to preach to them, Jonah decided to disobey God. Disobedience is never good by the way.

The story turns to the disobedient preacher running from God and he got on a boat that was shipping items from one place to another. Word of advice: you have to be careful who you allow on your boat. These sailors allowed Jonah on their boat, and because of Jonah's disobedience all hell breaks loose in their lives.

God sent a storm and nearly destroyed their boat and lives, but when they threw Jonah overboard the most amazing thing happened... the storm ceased. Curious to know why? Because the storm was never meant for the sailors but because they had Jonah on their boat, they experienced his storm. I have a question for you to ponder: who is in your boat that does not belong? Now, I am not suggesting that we should be throwing people overboard, but you do not have to allow subtractors and dividers to cause storms in your life. There are many ports that you can stop at and politely nudge them off your boat.

There are adders, subtractors, dividers and fourthly, the most rare and so important are the **multipliers**. Everyone needs a multiplier. These are people that take us to a whole new level. They are mentors - people who will pour into us. We need these people in our life. If you are curious how to attract a multiplier in your life the answer is one word: HONOR. Always remember that honor is the currency of the Kingdom of God.

FRIENDSHIP DEFINED

Back to friendship: What is a friend? Once, I went searching for different definitions of friendship and this is what I found through Google: "A friend is someone who knows how crazy you are, yet is still willing to be seen in public with you." Another definition says that a "friend is someone who comes over to your house and eats all your food and then uses all your stuff with his or her Cheeto hands without asking you." We all have a friend like that. But Proverbs 17:17 defines friendship like this, **"A friend loves at all times, and a brother is born for a time of adversity."** In life you need some friends who will always love you and be there during times of adversity. We all go through stuff. The Christian life was never meant to be lived alone. We all need friends in this life.

Unfortunately, today we are in desperate need of relationships. So many of us are relationally bankrupt. We have thousands of friends on Facebook and thousands of followers on Instagram, but no real friends in life. The enemy wants to isolate each of us. We are all by design relational beings created in the image of a relational God.

HOW TO ACTUALLY DO IT

Let me walk us through what a true friendship looks like according to the Bible. It is the relationship between David and Jonathan. This friendship is the model that I believe God wants us to base our relationships off of. If you remember the story, Saul was king of Israel and his son Jonathan was the heir to his throne. After David killed Goliath, Saul invited David to live at the King's palace. It was there that David and Jonathan developed a deep friendship, a brotherhood. The Bible tells the story in **1st Samuel 18:1-4: "After David had finished talking with Saul, Jonathan became one in spirit with David, and he loved him as himself. ² From that day Saul kept David with him and did not let him return home to his family. ³ And Jonathan made a covenant with David because he loved him as himself. ⁴ Jonathan took off the _robe_ he was wearing and gave it to David, along with his _tunic_, and even his _sword_, his _bow_ and his _belt_."** There are five items that Jonathan gave David that gives us a picture of what true Godly relationships look like. Jonathan gave David his robe, his tunic, his sword, his bow, and his belt. These 5 items illustrate the beautiful exchange that takes place in covenant relationships.

#1 THE ROBE

First, Jonathan gave David his robe. In ancient times, when you gave someone your robe, it meant, "Everything I have is yours." Or in other words, what is mine is yours (*mi casa es su casa*). Healthy friendships are based on GENEROSITY. In the early church, they sold all their possessions and shared with their brothers and sisters in Christ. They were in a covenant relationship together. I want to encourage you to be generous with your friends. Generosity is at the very heart of God. God loved us so much that He gave His only Son. Generosity is the action that breaks the back of greed in our life. God blesses those who are generous, because being generous is being like God. Whenever someone in your church community has a birthday, be generous and get them a gift card. If we want our relationships to produce a harvest, we have to sow seeds into them of generosity. Be generous with those you are in relationship with. But generosity in friendship goes beyond just buying gift cards for birthdays, it has to do with our time and our talent as well.

It is so easy for us in the busyness of life to forget to invest our time with our friends. If we want strong friendships, then we are going to have to spend time with them. Be generous with your talent in your friendships. When your friend is moving, use the talent you have to carry boxes and help them move. Nobody can carry those boxes like you, so instead of sleeping in on Saturday when your friend is moving, get up out of bed to use your time and your special talent of carrying boxes to help your friend out. If you want your friendships to grow, then you are going to have to invest in them. Jonathan was generous towards David.

#2 THE TUNIC (ARMOR)

The second thing that Jonathan gave was his tunic or his armor. The Hebrew word for tunic means armor. Without armor, a soldier becomes vulnerable. When Jonathan took off his armor he was saying, "I am going to take off my guard and show you the real me. I am going to be vulnerable with you." A real friendship means we take off the masks that we wear to church on Sunday so that everyone thinks we are perfect, and we become vulnerable and allow certain people to see our weaknesses and flaws. God is strong when we are vulnerable; God is strong when we are weak. God will not bless the pretend us; God will only bless the real us. Being real and being vulnerable is not a sign of weakness but it is a sign of strength. Just remember this right here: God is not looking for the ideal you, the perfect you, or the Instagram you; God is looking for the real you. Take off the mask and find some people you can become real with. I want to encourage you to get real and be vulnerable with your friends, for far too many Christians are as fake as a Kardashian. If you want to grow in your friendships, you have to be real. You cannot hide behind your armor.

#3 THE SWORD

The third item that Jonathan gave David was his sword. By doing this Jonathan was saying, "I will fight for you, but I will never fight against you. I will never use my sword to hurt you. I will never stab you in the back. I will serve you." This was an act of service. Healthy relationships are built on serving one another. Serving is a key to any relationship whether it is business, church, or family. If we think friendship is all about our friends serving us, then we are not going to have any friends at all. Friendship is a two-way street of serving one another. It is through serving one another that trust is developed and strengthened. Find ways to serve the people around you and watch what happens in your life. God will send the right friends along your path.

#4 THE BOW

The fourth item Jonathan gave to David was his bow. This bow represented protection. Jonathan was saying to David, "I will protect you." True friendship means we protect one another, and we defend each other. We will protect the reputation and even secrets of our friends. Lifelong friendships are based on protection. We must protect each other. We are stronger together than we are apart. There is power in unity. When you get some friends in your life, and I am talking about godly friends, they will cover you. They cover your marriage in prayer, they call you Sunday after church and ask why you missed. They will tell you buying that overpriced car probably is not the best decision. When we get real friends around us all of a sudden, we are protected where we are vulnerable. We need lifelong friendships to help cover us from the attacks of the enemy. Refuse to isolate, because we need friends in our life.

#5 THE BELT

The fifth and final item that Jonathan gave to David was his belt, that was what helped him hold his armor together. Ephesians 6 is where Paul discusses the armor of God and in **Ephesians 6:14** Paul says, "**Stand firm then, with the**

belt of truth buckled around your waist." In the Bible, the belt represents truth. When Jonathan gave his belt, he was promising David to always be honest. Strong relationships are built on honesty. You cannot build lasting relationships without honesty. Therefore, surround yourself with people who will tell you what you need to hear, not just what you want to hear. I am so glad I have a few friends in life who are willing to just tell me when I am being dumb. We need some friends who will not always agree with us and be willing to tell us when we are wrong. We need some friends who will just be real and honest with us. Otherwise, we will never see our blind spots in life.

CONCLUSION

The robe is a symbol of generosity, the armor is a symbol of being vulnerable, the sword is a symbol of trust and service, the bow is a symbol of protection, and the belt is a symbol of honesty. I want to challenge you to not just be a hearer of the Word but also a doer of the Word; to be generous, to be vulnerable, to be trusting, to protect, and to always be truthful. One time the legendary Dr. Billy Graham was asked what he would say was the one thing that brought about success in his life and ministry. He said the key to his success was that he found a group of friends he could grow old with. The key to the success in your life is finding a group of friends that you can grow old with as well. We need our friends and our friends need us. But for friendships to work we have to work them; we have to develop them.

ULTIMATE PRACTICAL GUIDE TO HAPPINESS

PT. 4

HOW TO OVERCOME ANXIETY & DEPRESSION

INTRODUCTION

Years ago, I heard about a woman who owned a pet hamster that was much like family to her, but one day she came home, and the hamster was lying on its back appearing to be dead. The woman wanted to make sure that her hamster was not in a coma, so she threw water on the hamster and it did not budge; the hamster still appeared to be dead. She then decided to take the hamster to the veterinarian and have it checked out. When the vet examined the hamster he said to the woman, "Your hamster is dead." The woman responded, "Well can you please run some tests just to make sure?" The vet honored the woman's request and brought in a cat for the first test. The cat grabbed the hamster and chewed on it and the hamster did not budge; the hamster seemed to be dead. The vet said, "Ma'am your hamster is dead." The woman began to cry and said, "Can you please run one final test just to make sure?" Once again, the vet honored the woman's request and brought in a Labrador dog for his final test. The Labrador put the hamster in its mouth and tossed the hamster around like a toy and it did not budge; the hamster appeared to be dead. The vet finally said, "Ma'am your hamster is dead and your bill is $5000." The woman panicked and shouted, "Are you kidding me, for what?" The vet responded, "I did a cat scan and a lab test therefore it will be $5000." The moral of the story is this: if you do not catch the simple things early on it will cost you a lot in the long run.

In life little things tend to make a huge difference. So often the smallest of things in life make the biggest of differences. I remember playing High School basketball and my coach would always say that the small things in practice would pay off the biggest during the game; he was right. In life nearly everyone wants to do big and great things. In fact, striving for greatness is one of the primary driving forces in our lives. It is that desire to succeed that causes you to set an alarm every morning to get out of bed and do what you do. We all want to succeed in our spiritual journey, our relationships, our finances, our health, and our happiness. Success is an innate desire that human beings are born with. But success is usually created with several small things rather than a few big things. In fact, what generally separates a good athlete from a great athlete or a good musician from a great musician is not talent but doing the little things consistently every week. Small things really do make a big difference in life. It is the things that no one sees behind the scenes that result in the things everyone wants in the spotlight.

THOUGHTS

One of the areas of our lives that we consider small but makes a big difference is our thought life. What are you thinking about? Your thought life is important. Your thoughts are powerful because your thoughts influence your words, and your words influence your actions, and your actions influence your habits, which ultimately creates your destiny. Your thoughts will either help or hinder your success in life. One of the best lessons you can learn is that your thoughts determine who you become.

**Proverbs 23:7 says,
"For as someone thinks in their heart, so are they."**

If you think life is bad and miserable it will probably be bad and miserable. But if you think that life is good and enjoyable then it will probably be good and enjoyable. Thomas Jefferson said, "Nothing can stop the man with the right mental attitude... nothing on earth can help the man with the wrong attitude." Your thoughts matter. Your thoughts shape your attitude. As the old saying goes, "Your attitude determines your altitude." The attitude you choose to adopt in life determines how you see the world. You can see the world through the window of positivity and faith or you can see the world through the window of negativity and fear.

Your thoughts and your attitude are the window in which you see the world. One Sunday, I brought a window on stage with me during a sermon I was delivering to illustrate the importance of attitude in life from a book I was reading called "Attitude is Everything" by Jeff Keller. In life we are all behind a window looking out. We are looking at people, we are looking at the news, and we are looking at life. But in our life things happen and dirt gets thrown on the window. Our thoughts and attitudes get a little muddied. We begin to see things differently.

We begin to become disappointed and frustrated. For example, think of your job. You start the job with a clear window and a good attitude but over time you allow your window to get dirty and all of a sudden you see things differently. Well, I should just quit my job. I do not like what I am seeing. You know the job may not be the problem. Maybe your window is dirty. Maybe your thoughts and attitude are not what they once were. Many of us are like this when it comes to church. You once had a great attitude and had good thoughts about church but because your window is dirty you think there is something wrong with the church. Can I make a suggestion before you end your marriage, before you quit your job, and before you leave your church? My suggestion is why not try cleaning the window first. Before you make some radical decisions, clean the window. I will guarantee you that you will see things differently.

Everyday there are buzzards and hummingbirds looking for food. The buzzard searches and searches for dead things and the buzzard will find the dead things. The hummingbird on the other hand searches and searches for sweet things and the hummingbird finds sweet things. In life there are positive things and there are negative things, sweet things and dead things. You have to make a decision whether or not you are a hummingbird or a buzzard because who you are is what you will find. If you are always finding the negative that probably means you are not a hummingbird. The good news is you can be transformed. Your thoughts and your attitudes in life matter; they are minor things that make a major difference. But too often our thoughts are dominated by negativity, fear, and anxiety.

Therefore, how do we fight this battle in the mind and win? Let us look at Elijah one last time. **1st Kings 19:1-2, "Now Ahab told Jezebel everything Elijah had done and how he had killed all the prophets with the sword. ² So Jezebel sent a messenger to Elijah to say, "May the gods deal with me, be it ever so severely, if by this time tomorrow I do not make your life like that of one of them."** King Ahab went home and told his wife Jezebel what took place on Mt. Carmel. He told her how Elijah slaughtered the 450 prophets of Baal and the 400 prophets of Asherah who had a seat at her table. When she heard this, she was furious and she decided to take over. As the saying goes, "Hell hath no fury like a woman scorned." Jezebel sent word to Elijah that by tomorrow he was a dead man. Now you would think that this would not faze Elijah at all. Elijah is the man of God; he is a man of great faith. You would think that but it is completely wrong.

1st Kings 19:3-4 says, "**Elijah was afraid and ran for his life. When he came to Beersheba in Judah, he left his servant there, ⁴ while he himself went a day's journey into the wilderness. He came to a broom bush, sat down under it and prayed that he might die. "I have had enough, Lord," he said. "Take my life; I am no better than my ancestors."**

When I read this passage, it absolutely shocks me. This is not the Elijah we read about. This is not the Elijah who went to Kerith where he was cut down yet fed by Ravens. This is not the Elijah that traveled 100 miles to Zarephath and found a widow who God would use to multiply a little bit of flower and oil to give them food. This is not the Elijah who called forth a dead boy back to life, which was the first time that had ever happened in the Bible. This is not the Elijah who would square off with 450 prophets of Baal and 400 prophets of Asherah and call down fire from heaven. What has happened to Elijah? This woman named Jezebel said, "I am going to kill you" and he literally had a full-blown panic attack. Elijah was depressed and suicidal. What was going on here?

For too long the church has been silent on the issue of mental and emotional health. In fact, I would say the church has produced a lot of damage here by condemning people who battle depression or other mental and emotional illnesses. Right now, America faces a mental and emotional health crisis. It is estimated that two-thirds of Americans face some form of depression, anxiety, or PTSD. This is not just an issue that teenage girls face when they get their heart broken. Depression is an issue that whether you are young or old, rich or poor you can face. Did you know it is possible to be a Christian and struggle with depression? I just want to tell you if you struggle in this area that it does not mean your faith is broken. Too often when people are fighting depression in Christian circles, they are told they have a lack of faith and many pastors have made things worse instead of better for those people.

Throughout the Bible there are many heroes who faced depression and even suicidal thoughts; Elijah was not the only one. Others include King David, Jonah, Isaiah, and Jeremiah who cried out to God and wished he had never even been born. In church history many of the greatest leaders struggled here such as Martin Luther, Charles Spurgeon, and even Mother Teresa. Depression is a real issue that many Christians face. But know this: God does not want you to be mentally and emotionally unhealthy.

HOW TO BECOME MENTALLY &EMOTIONALLY UNHEALTHY

Because this is such a real issue, I want to share with you some different ways that we can become mentally and emotionally unhealthy. So how do we reach that state in our lives? Let me give you three quick ways to find yourself fighting depression and anxiety.

#1 BURN THE CANDLE AT BOTH ENDS

The first way we reach mental and emotional unhealthiness is by wearing ourselves out. It said earlier that Elijah ran for his life to Beersheba. Elijah ran as far as he possibly could. Beersheba is the southern border of Israel. Mount Carmel, where Elijah fought the prophets of Baal is in Northern Israel. Beersheba is all the way down south. Elijah ran for his life and that journey physically wore him out. He was exhausted. When you drain yourself physically you will become unhealthy emotionally. There is an old Greek saying which says, "You will break the bow if you keep it always bent." You were not designed to constantly be on the go. It does not matter who you are. If you never stop to rest, you will burn out. I am not prophesying doom over your life, but I am telling you that if you do not stop to refuel your car it will run out of gas. Your body and soul and spirit are all interconnected. When your body is running on empty that means it will also impact your emotions and your mind. Depression is not always some kind of spiritual issue that is fighting demons off. Depression can be very real because you have worn yourself out. If you want to become mentally and emotionally unhealthy then just wear yourself out.

#2 REMOVE GOOD PEOPLE
FROM YOUR LIFE

Secondly, if you want to get depressed, then isolate yourself from other people. We saw that not only did Elijah run to Beersheba, but he left his servant behind. Meaning Elijah isolated himself. You were never created to be a hermit. You are a relational being created in the image of a relational God. We all need people in our lives.

#3 FORGET THE POSITIVE JUST
LOOK AT THE NEGATIVE

And thirdly, focus on the negative. In **verse 4** it says, "**while he himself went a day's journey into the wilderness. He came to a broom bush, sat down under it and prayed that he might die. "I have had enough, Lord," he said. "Take my life; I am no**

better than my ancestors." I am no better than my ancestors. He has succumbed to the Negative Nancy Syndrome. In that moment of Elijah's life self-pity took over. He forgot all about God's faithfulness. He forgot about the ravens at Kerith; he forgot about the supernatural provision at Zarephath; he forgot about God raising the widow's son back from the dead, and he forgot about God sending fire on Mount Carmel. His focus was not on the good things God had done, but his focus was on the negative thing Jezebel promised to do to him.

BECOMING MENTALLY & EMOTIONALLY HEALTHY

Elijah wore himself out, he removed himself from good people, and he focused on the negative instead of the positive. All of this resulted in severe depression and even suicidal thoughts. There is a real enemy out there. The enemy comes and attacks you between the ears; he attacks your mind and your thoughts. **Proverbs 23:7** says, "**For as someone thinks in their heart, so are they.**" Your thoughts matter. **Proverbs 4:23** says, "**Above all else, guard your heart, for everything you do flows from it.**" Guarding your heart is important. Whose responsibility is it to guard your heart? It is your job. It is not your husband's job or your wife's job. It is not your boyfriend or girlfriend's job. It is not your best friend's job or your pastor's job. It is not your boss's job or your teacher's job. It is your job to guard your heart. We oversee our own hearts. But so often we only focus on the outside of us instead of the inside of us. We make sure our hair looks good and that our teeth are white and clothes are sharp. We look great on the outside but inside we are a mess. We are a mess on the inside because we do not protect our hearts. We are better at protecting our cars than we are our hearts. Remember this: the enemy cannot take your joy or peace, but you can choose to give it to him. You give away your mental and emotional health by wearing yourself out, isolating yourself from people, and focusing on the negative in your life. But just as there are three ways to bring about depression there are three ways to fight it. God gave Elijah three different ways to become mentally and emotionally healthy again.

#1 TAKE CARE OF YOURSELF

The first way may shock you a little bit because it is not spiritual at all but very practical and that is to take care of your bod. **1st Kings 19:5-8** says, **"Then he lay down under the bush and fell asleep. All at once an angel touched him and said, "Get up and eat."** [6] **He looked around, and there by his head was**

some bread baked over hot coals, and a jar of water. He ate and drank and then lay down again. [7] The angel of the Lord came back a second time and touched him and said, "Get up and eat, for the journey is too much for you." [8] So he got up and ate and drank. Strengthened by that food, he traveled forty days and forty nights until he reached Horeb, the mountain of God." When Elijah was at his lowest battling depression God did not show up and rebuke him or preach at him and tell him he should pray more.

No, God said eat something and rest because the journey ahead of you is a long one. For some, the most spiritual thing you can do in the season of your life is to be intentional about taking care of yourself and rest. Why not try honoring the Sabbath? Take a rest and stop leading on empty. Not only do we want to rest from the busyness of life, we also need to be healthy with our diet and exercise. When you take care of yourself physically that means you will also feel better emotionally and spiritually. Find ways to get out and exercise. Go for a walk with your dog, take the stairs instead of the elevator. Be healthy. We do not just want to be healthy spiritually as Christians, but we want to be healthy in all areas and we do that by eating right and resting. Now that may not sound very spiritual but sometimes the most practical things are the most spiritual things you can do.

#2 BE AROUND GOOD PEOPLE

Secondly, be intentional to be around good people instead of isolating yourself. **Verses 9-10** say, **"There he went into a cave and spent the night. The Lord Appears to Elijah And the word of the Lord came to him: "What are you doing here, Elijah?"** [10] **He replied, "I have been very zealous for the Lord God Almighty. The Israelites have rejected your covenant, torn down your altars, and put your prophets to death with the sword. I am the only one left, and now they are trying to kill me too."** Elijah believed a lie from the enemy that he was all alone in Israel. He thought he was the only one left. God said to Elijah, "You are not the only one Elijah. In fact, there are 7000 people in Israel who have not bowed down to Baal." Elijah believed a lie that he was all alone. Can I just tell you that you are not all alone. There are others out there who are with you. It is so important that amid your Christian life that you get plugged into a group of believers. You need friendships in your life. **Isolation is the path to depression, but relationships are the path to joy**. Relationships really are the essence of life.

#3 ENTER THE PRESENCE OF GOD

God told Elijah in the midst of his depression to get up and go to Mount Horeb. This is the mountain of God. This is the mountain believed to be where God gave the Ten Commandments. This was the place you would meet with God. To avoid depression be sure to experience the presence of God, because in His presence there is the fullness of Joy and the Joy of the Lord is our strength. When you experience God's power in your life it will strengthen you. Instead of focusing on the negative you focus on God. Keep your eyes on Jesus who is the author and the finisher of your story. He who began a good work in you is faithful to complete it. Your negative circumstances do not define you. God has already defined you. God says you are His child created to be **HAPPY & HOLY.**

Helpful Books That I Recommend

The list below are the primary books that helped create this book that I highly recommend for future reading:

David: A Man Of Passion
Charles Swindoll

The Power Of Positive Thinking
Norman Vincent Peale

Christianity for Modern Pagans
Peter Kreeft

Desiring God
John Piper

Sacred Pathways
Gary Thomas

Elijah: A Man Of Heroism & Humility
by Charles Swindoll

The Problem Of Pain
C.S. Lewis

A Tale Of Three Kings
Gene Edwards

Attitude Is Everything
Jeff Keller

Moses: A Man Of Selfless Dedication
Charles Swindoll

www.ingramcontent.com/pod-product-compliance
Lightning Source LLC
Chambersburg PA
CBHW010938120626
46554CB00008B/2523